Building Excellence:
The Rewards and Challenges
of Integrating Research
into the Undergraduate
Curriculum

*Building Excellence: The Rewards and Challenges of Integrating
Research into the Undergraduate Curriculum* has been co-pub-
lished simultaneously as *Journal of Evidence-Based Social Work,*
Volume 4, Numbers 1/2 2007.

Building Excellence:
The Rewards and Challenges of Integrating Research into the Undergraduate Curriculum

Catherine N. Dulmus, PhD
Karen M. Sowers, PhD
Editors

Building Excellence: The Rewards and Challenges of Integrating Research into the Undergraduate Curriculum has been co-published simultaneously as *Journal of Evidence-Based Social Work, Volume 4, Numbers 1/2 2007.*

The Haworth Press, Inc.

www.HaworthPress.com

Building Excellence: The Rewards and Challenges of Integrating Research into the Undergraduate Curriculum has been co-published simultaneously as *Journal of Evidence-Based Social Work,* Volume 4, Numbers 1/2 2007.

The development, preparation, and publication of this work has been undertaken with great care. However, the publisher, employees, editors, and agents of The Haworth Press and all imprints of The Haworth Press, Inc., including The Haworth Medical Press® and Pharmaceutical Products Press®, are not responsible for any errors contained herein or for consequences that may ensue from use of materials or information contained in this work. Opinions expressed by the author(s) are not necessarily those of The Haworth Press, Inc. With regard to case studies, identities and circumstances of individuals discussed herein have been changed to protect confidentiality. Any resemblance to actual persons, living or dead, is entirely coincidental.

The Haworth Press is committed to the dissemination of ideas and information according to the highest standards of intellectual freedom and the free exchange of ideas. Statements made and opinions expressed in this publication do not necessarily reflect the views of the Publisher, Directors, management, or staff of The Haworth Press, Inc., or an endorsement by them.

Library of Congress Catalog-in-Publication Data

Building excellence: the rewards and challenges of integrating research into the undergraduate curriculum/ Catherine N. Dulmus, Karen M. Sowers, editors.
  p. cm.
  Includes bibliographical references and index.
  ISBN 13: 978-0-7890-3441-0 (hard cover : alk. paper)
  ISBN 13: 978-0-7890-3442-7 (soft cover : alk. paper)
  1. Universities and colleges–Curricula–United States. 2. Social work education–Curricula–United States. 3. Education, Higher–Aims and objectives–United States. I. Dulmus, Catherine N. II. Sowers, Karen M. (Karen Marlaine)
LB2361.5.B85 2008
378.1'99–dc22
                        2007015341

The HAWORTH PRESS Inc.

Abstracting, Indexing & Outward Linking

PRINT and ELECTRONIC BOOKS & JOURNALS

This section provides you with a list of major indexing & abstracting services and other tools for bibliographic access. That is to say, each service began covering this periodical during the the year noted in the right column. Most Websites which are listed below have indicated that they will either post, disseminate, compile, archive, cite or alert their own Website users with research-based content from this work. (This list is as current as the copyright date of this publication.)

Abstracting, Website/Indexing Coverage . . . . Year When Coverage Began

- *(IBR) International Bibliography of Book Reviews on the Humanities and Social Sciences (Thomson) <http://www.saur.de>* . . . 2006

- *(IBZ) International Bibliography of Periodical Literature on the Humanities and Social Sciences (Thomson) <http://www.saur.de>* 2006

- ***Academic Search Premier (EBSCO)** <http://search.ebscohost.com>* 2006

- ***CINAHL (Cumulative Index to Nursing & Allied Health Literature) (EBSCO)** <http://www.cinahl.com>* 2005

- ***CINAHL Plus (EBSCO)** <http://search.ebscohost.com>* 2006

- ***Social Services Abstracts (Cambridge Scientific Abstracts)** <http://www.csa.com>* 2004

- ***Social Work Abstracts (NASW)** <http://www.silverplatter.com/catalog/swab.htm>* 2006

- *Academic Source Premier (EBSCO) <http://search.ebscohost.com>* . . . 2007

(continued)

(continued)

Bibliographic Access

- *MediaFinder <http://www.mediafinder.com/>*

- *Ulrich's Periodicals Directory: The Global Source for Periodicals Information Since 1932 <http://www.bowkerlink.com>*

Special Bibliographic Notes related to special journal issues (separates) and indexing/abstracting:

- indexing/abstracting services in this list will also cover material in any "separate" that is co-published simultaneously with Haworth's special thematic journal issue or DocuSerial. Indexing/abstracting usually covers material at the article/chapter level.
- monographic co-editions are intended for either non-subscribers or libraries which intend to purchase a second copy for their circulating collections.
- monographic co-editions are reported to all jobbers/wholesalers/approval plans. The source journal is listed as the "series" to assist the prevention of duplicate purchasing in the same manner utilized for books-in-series.
- to facilitate user/access services all indexing/abstracting services are encouraged to utilize the co-indexing entry note indicated at the bottom of the first page of each article/chapter/contribution.
- this is intended to assist a library user of any reference tool (whether print, electronic, online, or CD-ROM) to locate the monographic version if the library has purchased this version but not a subscription to the source journal.
- individual articles/chapters in any Haworth publication are also available through the Haworth Document Delivery Service (HDDS).

As part of Haworth's continuing committment to better serve our library patrons, we are proud to be working with the following electronic services:

AGGREGATOR SERVICES

EBSCOhost

Ingenta

J-Gate

Minerva

OCLC FirstSearch

Oxmill

SwetsWise

Ingenta

MINERVA

FirstSearch

Oxmill Publishing

SwetsWise

LINK RESOLVER SERVICES

1Cate (Openly Informatics)

CrossRef

Gold Rush (Coalliance)

LinkOut (PubMed)

LINKplus (Atypon)

LinkSolver (Ovid)

LinkSource with A-to-Z (EBSCO)

Resource Linker (Ulrich)

SerialsSolutions (ProQuest)

SFX (Ex Libris)

Sirsi Resolver (SirsiDynix)

Tour (TDnet)

Vlink (Extensity, *formerly Geac*)

WebBridge (Innovative Interfaces)

 Gold Rush

 LinkOut.

 atypon

O V I D LinkSolver

 ULRICH'S RESOURCE LINKER

SFX

SerialsSolutions

 SirsiDynix

TOUR

extensity

  WebBridge

ABOUT THE EDITORS

Catherine N. Dulmus, PhD, is Associate Dean for Research and Director of the Buffalo Center for Social Research in the School of Social Work at the University at Buffalo. From 1999-2005 she was on the faculty of the College of Social Work at The University of Tennessee where she taught in the undergraduate social work program. She received her baccalaureate degree in Social Work from Buffalo State College in 1989, the Master's Degree in Social Work from University at Buffalo in 1991 and the PhD degree in Social Welfare from the University at Buffalo in 1999. Dr. Dulmus' research focuses on child mental health, prevention, and violence. She has authored or coauthored several journal articles, 7 books, and has presented her research nationally and internationally. Dr. Dulmus is founding co-editor of the *Journal of Evidence-Based Social Work*, founding co-editor of *Best Practices in Mental Health: An International Journal*, associate editor of *Stress, Trauma, and Crisis: An International Journal*, and sits on the editorial boards of the *Journal of Human Behavior in the Social Environment* and *Victims and Offenders Journal*. In 2002 was awarded an excellence in teaching citation from the University of Tennessee. Prior to obtaining the PhD, her social work practice background encompassed almost a decade of experience in the fields of mental health and school social work.

Karen M. Sowers, PhD, Guest Editor, was appointed Professor and Dean of the College of Social Work at the University of Tennessee, Knoxville in August 1997. She served as Director of the School of Social Work at Florida International University from June 1994 to August 1997 and as the Undergraduate Program Director of the School of Social Work at Florida International University from 1986 to 1994. She received her baccalaureate degree in Sociology from the University of Central Florida in 1974, the Master's Degree in Social Work from Florida State University in 1977 and the PhD in Social Work from Florida State University in 1986.

Dr. Sowers is nationally known for her research and scholarship in the areas of international practice, juvenile justice, child welfare, cultural diversity and culturally effective intervention strategies for social work practice, and social work education. Her current research and community interests include the development of initiatives to support responsible and involved fatherhood, the implementation and evaluation of community-oriented policing, international social work practice and juvenile justice practice. She has authored or co-authored numerous books, book chapters and refereed journal articles. She has served as a founding editorial board member of the *Journal of Research on Social Work Practice*, founding co-editor of *Best Practices in Mental Health: An International Journal* and is currently serving on the editorial boards of the *Journal of Evidence-Based Social Work: Advances in Practice, Programs, Research and Policy* and *Journal of Stress, Trauma and Crisis: An International Journal*.

Building Excellence:
The Rewards and Challenges
of Integrating Research
into the Undergraduate

CONTENTS

Foreword

I am pleased to provide the Foreword for this special volume. The national call for research institutions of higher learning to adopt a new model of baccalaureate education to strengthen critical thinking, independent thinking and creative imagination inspired us at UT. Believing that the university should be a special kind of intellectual environment we embarked on a journey to develop UT into an intellectual ecosystem and a community of learners. For the past several years The University of Tennessee, Knoxville has engaged in an effort to strengthen the undergraduate research experience as part of this effort. Numerous opportunities now exist at the University for undergraduate students. Research and creative projects give students professional experience in their chosen fields of interest and strongly enhance the educational experiences of talented and motivated students. These efforts have created a strong connection between undergraduate study and the creation of knowledge, allowing baccalaureate students to become active participants in collaborative learning experiences. Our goal is to develop into a student-centered research university in which faculty and students are mutual learners and researcher, interacting in a healthy and flourishing intellectual environment. This process has required change at all levels of the institution. Individual academic units have engaged in change at the level of the academic discipline–from strengthening research content in the curricula to providing new interdisciplinary research opportunities. Academic and administrative leaders at UT have given the undergraduate research initiative a high priority. Budgets at all levels of the institution have been realigned to support these new endeavors. Below are some examples of university-wide programs designed to engage faculty, baccalaureate students, and graduate students, in the enterprise of creating new knowledge.

[Haworth co-indexing entry note]: "Foreword." Crabtree, Dr. Loren. Co-published simultaneously in *Journal of Evidence-Based Social Work* (The Haworth Press, Inc.) Vol. 4. No. 1/2, 2007, pp. xix-xxi; and: *Building Excellence: The Rewards and Challenges of Integrating Research into the Undergraduate Curriculum* (ed: Catherine N. Dulmus, and Karen M. Sowers) The Haworth Press, Inc., 2007, pp. xv-xvii. Single or multiple copies of this article are available for a fee from The Haworth Document Delivery Service [1-800-HAWORTH 9:00 a.m. - 5:00 p.m. (EST). E-mail address: docdelivery@haworthpress.com].

Life of the Mind. All incoming freshmen engage in the "Life of the Mind Book Program" as part of the academic orientation at UTK. Students read an assigned book over the summer and participate in a group discussion of the book during orientation week. The goal is to create a shared intellectual context for incoming students, to stimulate discussion and interaction, and to cultivate the skills of critical thinking, reading, and engagement with ideas. Through its shared reading experience and common topics of conversation, the program offers an opportunity to interact with faculty and other first-year students before classes begin.

Academic Unit Research Activities. All academic units at UTK were challenged to develop unique research and creative activity opportunities for baccalaureate students. Examples include undergraduate summer research fellowships in chemistry, summer research biogeochemical internships to help foster a foundation in biotechnology, bioremediation and environmental engineering in South Africa, summer research stipends in psychology, and the development of "The Science Alliance" program to sponsor summer undergraduate research initiatives. In social work, the undergraduate curriculum has been redesigned to strengthen critical thinking, research methodology, and evidence-based practice. All social work seniors are required to conduct an original community-based research project under the guidance of a faculty mentor and present their research findings at the Exhibition of Undergraduate Research.

The Exhibition of Undergraduate Research and Creative Achievement. Each spring the University hosts an exhibition and competition for original research and creative works by its undergraduate students. It provides an opportunity for all students engaged in original and creative work to exhibit their works and compete in 16 different discipline-based divisions. The Exhibition not only recognizes the important achievements of its participants, but also celebrates the importance placed on individualized work as a vital component of the educational process. It further honors faculty who have given generously of their time and resources to serve as mentors for students who have sought exceptional learning opportunities. Awards for outstanding research are generously funded by the Office of Research, University Honors Program, and The University of Tennessee chapter of Phi Kappa Phi National Honor Society.

The University of Tennessee/Oak Ridge National Laboratory Chancellor's Summer Research Internship Program. The university honors program and Oak Ridge National Laboratory (ORNL) sponsor a summer internship program to promote research and creative activity among undergraduate students. All undergraduate students enrolled at UT are eligible to apply. The program consists of two parts. The first part of the program, funded by the Chancellor's Office, funds up to 15 internships at $2,000 each for the summer to support students who each work on a research or creative project with a faculty mentor for two months of the summer. In addition, each intern has tuition and fees paid for two hours of independent study course credit. The purpose of the internships is to increase the participation of UT undergraduate students in the research enterprise. Faculty mentors provide guidance in the choice of a proj- ect and in the practice of professional approaches and methods. The role of the faculty mentor is critical to the success of the program, and faculty who are involved with an intern receive an honorarium of $500. Students are expected to be involved in actual scholarly work independent of a classroom setting. The second part of the program, sponsored and administered by the UT Honors Program is funded by ORNL which funds up to 15 internships for students to work directly at the laboratory site with professional researchers of the Laboratory. These internships carry a stipend of $2000 for two months work at ORNL.

The article by Frank Spicuzza, Director of the undergraduate social work program at UT provides an example of how one academic unit can advance research and creative activity opportunities for baccalaureate students. The College of Social Work at UT has provided leadership within their own programs and throughout the university in our move to provide all interested undergraduate students with experiences to engage in inquiry, critical thinking, original thought, and collaborative, interdisciplinary learning.

Dr. Loren Crabtree, Chancellor
The University of Tennessee, Knoxville

Preface

The Boyer Report and the Council on Social Work Education have placed expectations on universities and social work programs to strategically strengthen the research curriculum and experience at the undergraduate level. How can undergraduate social work programs respond to this emerging push to educate undergraduate students to develop, use, and communicate empirically-based knowledge? This special volume provides an overview of the undergraduate research movement and specifically highlights one social work program's progress and challenges toward that end. We hope that lessons learned from this program can be informative and instrumental to other programs embarking on this challenging and rewarding endeavor. This collection also showcases examples of research conducted by undergraduate students at the University of Tennessee (UT) College of Social Work. Each of these was conducted by seniors and entered in the Undergraduate Research Exhibition at the university. For the purposes of this collection, upon graduation each researcher was paired with a doctoral student in the UT College of Social Work to assist the researcher in placing their research in publication form. The research is the sole work of the undergraduate students.

We are especially pleased that Dr. Loren Crabtree, Chancellor of the University of Tennessee, Knoxville has written the Foreword to this volume. It is his vision and leadership which has provided the facilitating conditions for undergraduate students to have opportunities to engage in meaningful research at UT. Dr. William Rowe provides an especially useful introductory article which frames the history of this movement as well as helping us understand the critical need for strengthening research

[Haworth co-indexing entry note]: "Preface." Dulmus, Catherine N., and Karen M. Sowers. Co-published simultaneously in *Journal of Evidence-Based Social Work* (The Haworth Press, Inc.) Vol. 4, No. 1/2, 2007, pp. xxii-xxiv; and: *Building Excellence: The Rewards and Challenges of Integrating Research into the Undergraduate Curriculum* (ed: Catherine N. Dulmus, and Karen M. Sowers) The Haworth Press, Inc., 2007, pp. xix-xx. Single or multiple copies of this article are available for a fee from The Haworth Document Delivery Service [1-800-HAWORTH 9:00 a.m. - 5:00 p.m. (EST). E-mail address: docdelivery@haworthpress.com].

at the undergraduate level. Mr. Frank J. Spicuzza, the unfailing and re-sourceful Director of the Undergraduate Social Work Program at the University of Tennessee shares valuable insights into the obstacles, challenges and rewards of building a meaningful undergraduate social work research experience. This volume concludes with a particularly thoughtful article by Julia M. Watkins, Executive Director of the Council on Social Work Education, as she visions undergraduate research as critical to practice and preparation for advanced social work education.

For those students who allowed us to showcase their work in this special collection, a special thanks. We heard time and again from you and the doctoral student you were paired with as to what a positive educational experience writing for publication was and how much you learned from the peer-review process. A special thanks also to those colleagues from across the country who served as our guest reviewers. The feedback you provided students was invaluable in the learning process.

We acknowledge and pay special tribute to all of the undergraduate social work students who helped us build a valuable, meaningful research program. Your enthusiasm, diligence and partnership in this process has been . . . well, in your words . . . JUST AWESOME! And we thank you.

Catherine N. Dulmus, PhD
Karen M. Sowers, PhD

The Revitalization of Traditional University Values Leading to Undergraduate Research

William Rowe, DSW

SUMMARY. In response to the Boyer Report, research universities across the United States have begun to enhance research opportunities for undergraduate students. Such an educational opportunity imbues students with the urge for inquiry and a passion for problem solving that results in students who have the skills and experience necessary to supply the scientific, technological, academic, political, and creative leadership for the future. This article provides an overview of the Boyer Report and its application to undergraduate social work education, advocating that it is critical that social work take a central role in what has become a clear priority for America's top research universities. doi:10.1300/J394v04 n01_01 *[Article copies available for a fee from The Haworth Document Delivery Service: 1-800-HAWORTH. E-mail address: <docdelivery@haworth press.com> Website: <http://www.HaworthPress.com> © 2007 by The Haworth Press, Inc. All rights reserved.]*

KEYWORDS. Boyer Report, undergraduate education, social work education, research

---

William Rowe is Professor and Director, School of Social Work, University of South Florida, 4202 East Fowler Avenue MGY132, Tampa, FL 33620 (E-mail: mrowe@ chumal.cas.usf.edu).

[Haworth co-indexing entry note]: "The Revitalization of Traditional University Values Leading to Undergraduate Research." Rowe, William. Co-published simultaneously in *Journal of Evidence-Based Social Work* (The Haworth Press, Inc.) Vol. 4, No. 1/2, 2007, pp. 1-9; and: *Building Excellence: The Rewards and Challenges of Integrating Research into the Undergraduate Curriculum* (ed: Catherine N. Dulmus, and Karen M. Sowers) The Haworth Press, 2007, pp. 1-9. Single or multiple copies of this article are available for a fee from The Haworth Document Delivery Service [1-800-HAWORTH, 9:00 a.m. - 5:00 p.m. (EST). E-mail address: docdelivery@haworthpress.com].

Available online at http://jebsw.haworthpress.com
doi:10.1300/J394v04n01_01

INTRODUCTION

Most American colleges and universities have had substantial general education and core programs in the past. With the huge expansion of postsecondary Education systems and enrollments, there was a coincidental liberalization of higher education giving students a great deal more freedom of choice. Programs began to emphasize vocational and professional preparation versus core academic values.

The Carnegie Foundation for Advancement of Teaching published Missions of the College Curriculum in 1977 which suggested that undergraduate curriculum had become fragmented and incoherent and called for the revival of core and general education programs. Books like Bloom's *Closing of the American Mind* [1987] and D'Souza's *Illiberal Education* [1991] pointed to students declining levels of knowledge and analytical skills.

The Boyer Commission on Educating Undergraduate Students in the Research University was created in 1995 under the auspices of the Carnegie Foundation for Advancement of Teaching. It was felt that the freshman year had too often been reduced to remediation or repetition of high school curricula rather than an introduction to a new and broader arena of learning, and that both students and parents had developed their own ideas about education and credentialing rather than embracing traditional models. Dr. Boyer himself died after the second meeting but the commissioners continued to discourse, debate and produce writings that culminated in the Boyer Commission Report of 1998. This report was entitled *Reinventing Undergraduate Education: A Blueprint for America's Research Universities* (Boyer, 1998).

The report contained important and too many somewhat provocative elements. The commission's report was also referred to as an academic Bill of Rights. In the report they refer to both the student and the college having an obligation to the educational enterprise, in fact they went on to assert that: By admitting a student, any college or university commits itself to provide maximal opportunities for intellectual and creative development. These should include:

1. Opportunities to learn through inquiry rather than simple transmission of knowledge.
2. Training in the skills necessary for oral and written communication at levels that will serve the student both within the university and in postgraduate professional and personal life.

3. Appreciation of arts, humanities, sciences, and social sciences, and the opportunity to experience them at any intensity and depth the student can accommodate.
4. Careful and comprehensive preparation for whatever may lie beyond graduation, whether it be graduate school, professional school, or first professional position. (Boyer, 1998)

The student in a research university, however, has these additional rights:

1. Expectation of and opportunity for work with talented senior researchers to help and guide the student's efforts.
2. Access to first-class facilities in which to pursue research–laboratories, libraries, studios, computer systems, and concert halls.
3. Many options among fields of study and directions to move within those fields, including areas and choices not found in other kinds of institutions.
4. Opportunities to interact with people of backgrounds, cultures, and experiences different from the student's own and with pursuers of knowledge at every level of accomplishment, from freshmen students to senior research faculty. (Boyer, 1998)

In essence the research university owes every student an integrated educational experience in which the totality is deeper and more comprehensive than can be measured by simply earned credits. This educational experience will imbue students with the urge for inquiry and a passion for problem solving. This experience will also produce students with great communication skills, who are informed by their many different college experiences. The graduates produced through this educational experience will have the skills and experience necessary to supply the scientific, technological, academic, political, and creative leadership for the future.

Secondly, the report recommended 10 ways to change undergraduate education:

1. *Make Research-Based Learning the Standard.* It was suggested that the university's responsibility to provide the most productive context in which new ideas could be formed, that most new knowledge is formed out of group efforts, and it is rarely the case that an idea would be fully-developed from a single person. Universities must make research-based learning a priority so that undergraduate students may be provided with the best possible

learning environment. Students and professors should be able to work together and learn from each other through the use of research-based learning.

II. *Construct an Inquiry-Based Freshman Year.* An undergraduate students' first year should be a time for new stimulation and intellectual growth, and should not be taught as if it were another year of high school curricula.

III. *Build on the Freshman Foundation.* The freshman year inquiry-based learning experience must be extended into the following undergraduate years. The research university education must include Inquiry-based learning, collaborative experience, writing and speaking expectations throughout these years. It is also very important to make sure that students who enter the research university after the freshman year are smoothly integrated into this unique learning experience.

IV. *Remove Barriers to Interdisciplinary Education.* Research universities must promote interdisciplinary undergraduate education, and remove any barriers that would keep it from being possible.

V. *Link Communication Skills and Course Work.* Undergraduate education must teach students strong communication skills, and in so doing create graduates who are skilled in both verbal and written communication.

VI. *Use Information Technology Creatively.* Because research universities create technological innovations, their students should have the opportunity to learn how to use new technology and apply it to their undergraduate years in order to learn more effectively.

VII. *Culminate with a Capstone Experience.* The final semester(s) should focus on a major project that uses all of the inquiry-based learning skills that the students learned in earlier years and a final integrative expression that utilizes these skills.

VIII. *Educate Graduate Students as Apprentice Teachers.* Research universities must prepare graduate students so that they are better equipped for teaching undergraduate students and other professional roles. They must also cultivate and facilitate the mentorship experience.

IX. *Change Faculty Reward Systems.* Research universities must validate their commitment to this new learning structure by changing the faculty reward system to something that compensates faculty for working with undergraduate students at the research level. Involvement with undergraduate students in the research experiences must be viewed as a value rather than a burden.

X. *Cultivate a Sense of Community.* Research universities should foster a learning community. Large universities must find ways to make students feel like they are part of a community and have a sense of belonging. Universities must also find ways for students to develop smaller communities within the larger university so they feel connected and important.

It is the center at Stony Brook University that has taken leadership in promoting these recommendations and coordinating regional meetings where interested representatives from interested universities discuss the challenges and successes in moving towards these goals. Currently there is an annual undergraduate research conference that showcases the best results of undergraduate research projects from across the nation (www.cur.org). Numerous research universities have embraced the concept with fully established undergraduate research offices that provide funding to both faculty and students for undergraduate research projects and many have included this in their quality enhancement programs and reaffirmation exercises (Chelimsky, 1997).

This was the case at the University of South Florida during the Southern Association of Colleges (SAC) reaffirmation exercise. Two broad-based university committees were established; One committee to revitalize the general education curriculum, and the other to recommend a program of undergraduate research. The general education committee focused on, not just ensuring that each of the courses are loaded with the skills needed for inquiry-based learning, but that the learning culture in the courses would promote such an atmosphere. In essence, the goal of the general education curriculum is to ensure that students have the skills needed for inquiry-based learning. These are not limited to, but include critical thinking, ethical analysis, cultural competence, and the principles of rational discourse among others. This transformation is very important, because the general education program is the foundation of a high-quality undergraduate education (USF, 2005). Moving the general education courses in this direction is seen as a multiyear process that requires both leadership and support. By revitalizing the general education curriculum the university is able to create a challenging intellectual environment that will help to attract the very best undergraduate students to become involved in the university's research endeavors (USF, 2005).

The second broad-based university committee established was the Undergraduate Research Committee (URC), which was drawn from many different faculty and academic administrators from several different colleges and campuses at the University of South Florida (USF, 2005). This committee came up with a recommended program for undergraduate research with five main points of consensus:

1. Research experiences will be available to all students in all disciplines.
2. Different types (levels of intensity) of research experience will be available to students based on their aptitude, ability, and interest.
3. Students at all levels–freshman through senior–should have opportunities to participate in research. Special efforts must be made to include traditionally underrepresented groups.
4. The undergraduate research experience can be divided into two main categories–inquiry-based and experience-based:

    a. The general education curriculum should ensure an inquiry-based experience for all undergraduate students.
    b. The URC will prepare more specific direction and guidance for the experience-based undergraduate research program.

5. Experience-based research is more than observation and information gathering. Research in this context ...

    a. Is engaging
    b. Is exciting
    c. Is enjoyable
    d. Involves analysis, original or creative thinking
    e. Leads to a product/outcome that can be shared

The first task of the undergraduate research committee was to determine the degree to which undergraduate research was already taking place in university. As it turned out, there were a great number of projects and activities under way. Clearly, there was more undergraduate research involvement in some disciplines than others. Building on the preparation of the general education curriculum, the research committee was to ensure that there was at least one undergraduate research requirement in all disciplines. Subsequently, the office of undergraduate research would offer a matching/mentorship program that would allow the opportunity for interested students and faculty to participate in a research experience. In some cases, these were research activities that were already underway. In other instances students would be matched up based on interest either during the semester or for the summer session. At the next level, the undergraduate research office would offer financial support for students and faculty to participate in guided research activities. These research activities may result in presenting what the results of the research or creative works were, and ultimately a co-authorship or significant contribution to the finished product. The work might be presented at university research conferences as a poster session or at a state or national conference.

The URC identified that certain opportunities would emerge from an institutional commitment to undergraduate research. Some of these included an institutional cultural shift; incentives for students, faculty, and departments; preparation for graduate education and research based careers and increased national visibility in attracting prospective students. At the same time, institutional barriers to the implementation of an undergraduate research initiative were identified that included traditional institutional culture; funding constraints; lack of infrastructure and lack of support. While many concerns were raised about infrastructure and resources, the university made a ten year funding commitment which included faculty and student incentive funds, departmental augmentation funds, dissemination funds, a freshman reading program, and a distinguished lecture series.

In many ways, the work begun by the Boyer commission, furthered by the reinvention center, and now embraced by a large number of American universities is in essence attempting to answer the question, what will be the qualitative difference for students attending a large research university as opposed to a primarily teaching institution? The answer in a simple way could be that the student, in light of the academic Bill of Rights, would have the opportunity to engage in meaningful research activities. These research activities are very important, because they allow students to learn through inquiry instead of simply passively receiving facts and concepts (USF, 2005). Through their participation in undergraduate research, students can learn many necessary skills to continue their lifetime learning process. These research experiences can also help undergraduate students develop a greater appreciation for the arts, humanities, sciences, and social sciences. Through the research process the student is able to learn how to frame important questions in a thoughtful manner and create new knowledge. This research process can be used by the student later in life to form a model for a lifetime of problem solving skills (USF, 2005). This research experience is also beneficial to an undergraduate student's future career plans.

The undergraduate college experience is a time of discovery, where students are given the opportunity to explore multiple career options. Undergraduate research practice gives the student some hands on experience and a chance to make a better informed decision about his or her future career plans. Working on an undergraduate research project also gives the students the opportunity to publish their work or present it in a professional context. This is an experience that can provide them with a competitive edge when applying to graduate school or an information based career (USF, 2005). The undergraduate research experience is also a great way to help college faculty learn more also. The Council on Undergraduate Research believes that undergraduate research is helpful to faculty because their involvement keeps them active in research and enhances their teaching and contribution to society (CUR, 2005).

Some disciplines, especially engineering, business, and the health sciences already have a great deal of experience in undergraduate research activities. The social sciences have less and humanities virtually none. The humanities historically have concentrated on the use of doctoral students in their research endeavors. Social work is in the unique position to demonstrate leadership in this revitalized interest in undergraduate research. Our students have been involved in volunteer activities, service learning and internships as a matter of course. In many cases, they are engaged in direct observation or collecting data on distress in communities and disadvantaged groups. This information is used as the basis for papers and proposals for both program development and knowledge building. Some schools of social work have already engaged in the undergraduate research process, and demonstrated excellent results alongside other social sciences and the traditional disciplines in the university. Social work educators would be extremely wise to seize this opportunity to take a central role in what has become a clear priority for America's top research universities.

REFERENCES

Bloom, A. (1987). *Closing of the American Mind.* New York: Simon and Schuster.
Boyer Commission on Educating Undergraduates in the Research University. (1998). *Reinventing Undergraduate Education: A Blueprint for America's Research Universities.* Stony Brook, NY: State University of New York at Stony Brook.

Carnegie Foundation for the Advancement of Teaching. (1997). *Missions of the College Curriculum*. Jossey-Bass, Inc.: San Francisco, CA.

Chelimsky, E. (1997). The coming transformations in Evaluation. *Evaluation for the 21st century. A Handbook*. Thousand Oaks, CA: Sage Publications, Inc.

Council on Undergraduate Research. (2005). *About CUR*. Retrieved May 4, 2005, from www.cur.org

D'Souza, D. (1991). *Illiberal education: the politics of race and sex on campus*. New York: Vintage Books.

USF Quality Enhancement Plan Committee. (2005). *INSPIRE: Infusing and Nurturing the Skills and Practice of Inquiry and Research in Education*. Tampa, FL: University of South Florida.

doi:10.1300/J394v04n01_01

An Undergraduate Social Work Program's Research Initiative: Evolution to a Culture of Inquirers

Frank J. Spicuzza, MSSW

SUMMARY. This article reports how one undergraduate social work program responded to the Boyer Commission's recommendations and the Council on Social Work Education's expectations to educate and train undergraduate students to develop, use, and communicate empirically-based knowledge. Discussion of the gradual development of an undergraduate research initiative includes the program's ideology and ambitions, administrative support, curricular changes, major challenges, crucial decisions and revisions, and student success. Assessment of the research initiative is highlighted with attention given to the utilization of collected data for revisions. Findings consistently indicate faculty mentoring of students is crucial to this effort. The article concludes with the author's hope that shared information regarding this program's research initiative will stimulate discussion and further thinking on preparing undergraduate social work students to be critical consumers and capable producers of studies pertinent to social work practice. doi:10.1300/J394v04n01_02 *[Article copies available for a fee from The Haworth Document Delivery Service: 1-800-HAWORTH. E-mail address: <docdelivery@*

Frank J. Spicuzza is affiliated with The University of Tennessee, College of Social Work, 302 Henson Hall, Knoxville, TN 37996 (E-mail: fspicuzz@utk.edu).

[Haworth co-indexing entry note]: "An Undergraduate Social Work Program's Research Initiative: Evolution to a Culture of Inquirers." Spicuzza, Frank J. Co-published simultaneously in *Journal of Evidence-Based Social Work* (The Haworth Press, Inc.) Vol. 4, No. 1/2, 2007, pp. 11-25; and: *Building Excellence: The Rewards and Challenges of Integrating Research into the Undergraduate Curriculum* (ed: Catherine N. Dulmus, and Karen M. Sowers) The Haworth Press, 2007, pp. 11-25. Single or multiple copies of this article are available for a fee from The Haworth Document Delivery Service [1-800-HAWORTH, 9:00 a.m. - 5:00 p.m. (EST). E-mail address: docdelivery@haworthpress.com].

11

KEYWORDS. Undergraduate research, research initiative, undergraduate social work education, curriculum development

INTRODUCTION

The undergraduate research initiative has become the jewel in the crown for the Baccalaureate of Science in Social Work (BSSW) Program at The University of Tennessee (UT). This gem was not developed overnight, rather it was a process that began with small incremental steps and has mushroomed into a significant component of the academic experience for undergraduate social work students. Collins and Porras (1997) in *Built to Last: Successful Habits of Visionary Companies* stress that often organizations stumble into unexpected opportunities that eventually grow into a significant, phenomenal success. These authors go on to say that organizations "make some of their best moves by experimentation, trial and error, and–quite literally–accident" (p. 9). This was the reality for the undergraduate research initiative. It did not come about by brilliant foresight and complex strategic planning but rather by trying new ideas, keeping those that work, and discarding those that were unsuccessful. Today the research initiative looks carefully planned, but it actually is an outcome of an evolutionary process that is still in process.

The research initiative evolved over a number of years due to UT BSSW program's willingness to seize opportunities consistent with its core ideology. The program has a penchant for not sitting still in its quest to better prepare students for the challenges of social work practice and graduate education. There is a commitment to prepare students for generalist practice, leadership in the profession, and for advanced study. A distinctive feature that sets the tone in the program is the persistence to excel. From its early beginning, the program has been consistent in its belief–there is always a better way to prepare students for a rapidly changing, complex world. Good is seen as not good enough. A constant stream of change has reset higher challenges in such areas as interactive learning, an evidence-based curriculum, outcomes assessment, and leadership development. Quality has always been and continues to be the paramount concern. Faculty and staff hired for the program have aligned with the ideas of educational excellence and a relentless drive to progress or they have left due to discomfort in this type of environment. It is within this context the undergraduate research initiative commenced and is continuously strengthened today. Yes, it can be said the program was in the right place at the right time for this initiative. It is safe to say, however, this was a program predisposed to taking risks, making changes, and enduring mistakes in pursuit of excellence that seized the presented opportunities. The opportunities matched with the program's ideology and ambitions. The program took small steps and gave undergraduate research a try.

The purpose of this paper is not to extol the importance of research in undergraduate social work education or to provide a history of The University of Tennessee involvement in undergraduate research, but rather to identify what has worked and what has not worked in a BSSW program as it implemented and gradually developed a research initiative. The paper will focus on crucial decisions and ignore minor tweaking.

RESOURCE ALLOCATION

Faculty and administrative support is essential to initiate and to continuous develop a research initiative. The faculty in the BSSW program and the dean of the College of Social Work have been and continue to be firmly committed to evidence-based social work. There is concern that the profession has neglected far too long studying the effectiveness of social work services. Being a compassionate, intuitive social worker with strong beliefs in service and altruism is not sufficient. Social workers need to base their practice upon recognized evidence-based knowledge. With the dean's support, BSSW program faculty have demonstrated a steadfast resolve to educate and train future social workers to be critical consumers and capable producers of studies pertaining to client needs and issues as well as service processes and outcomes. As this paper will identify, this resoluteness has lead to curricular revision, new assignments, faculty workload decisions, IRB and agency issues, and outcome assessment procedures. Without question, the continuous financial support from the dean's office has been instrumental in surging this initiative forward. From providing textbooks to field instructors that focus on the importance of research to social work practice to the recent purchase of a state-of-the-art poster printer to enhance students' entries in the

University's Exhibition of Undergraduate Research and Creative Achievement, the dean's office has generously provided what was needed to promote undergraduate research and scholarship.

CURRICULUM DEVELOPMENT

At the core of the BSSW program is a relentless, creative drive to provide a unique, challenging undergraduate learning experience for students. This drive along with the influence of the Council on Social Work Education revised accreditation standards and procedures (2003) and the Boyer's Commission's recommendations for research universities (1998) influenced faculty to strengthen the quality of the program's research component. Being a critical consumer of research was a noble goal, but it was not enough. The program set a higher standard, a research trained undergraduate social work student–a student who could develop, use, and communicate empirically based knowledge. As indicated in the Boyer Report (1998) the hope was to "turn the prevailing undergraduate culture of receivers into a culture of inquirers" (p. 16).

An opportunity for original research under the guidance of faculty is the most visible component of the BSSW program's research initiative. However, the foundation of the initiative was the work of the BSSW Curriculum Committee and the subsequent changes in course content and assignments. When the decision was made to require a research project for all students, the BSSW Curriculum Committee decided to review the entire curriculum for research content and skill development. The committee's analysis of all required course work resulted in research information being developmentally presented throughout the curriculum from the introduction course in social work to the senior capstone course, the Integrative Seminar. For example, the introduction course acquaints students with the scientific method and the importance of practice-effectiveness research to the profession. Subsequent courses address how to search for valid, reliable evidence; question and analyze scholarly information through the process of critical thinking; incorporate the profession's ethical principles in research efforts; formulate a practice-related research question; and finally conduct, implement, and present research that pertains to issues and needs of various client groups. Chart 1 identifies required BSSW courses and provides an example of a research-related topic addressed in each course.

Within a two year period, research and critical thinking became common denominators in every required social work course. With the expectation

CHART 1

Course	Topic
SW 200-Introduction to Social Work	scientific method and importance of research to practice
SW 250-Social Welfare	critical thinking skills in program evaluation
SW 310-Social Work Research	research design, methods, data analysis
SW 312-Social Work Practice I	identification of practice fallacies and judicious use of current best evidence
SW 313-Social Work Practice II	research applications to case management and crisis intervention
SW 314-Human Behavior and the Social Environment	evaluation of traditional theories about human behavior and development
SW 316-Culturally Responsive Social Work Practice	practice and research concerning multicultural issues
SW 380, 480, 481-Field Practice I, II, and III	reflective and critical thinking skills in discussing field practice experiences
SW 412-Social Work Practice III	field agency-based research
SW 416-Social Welfare Policies and Issues	research finding in proposing policy implementation and reform
SW 460-Integrative Seminar	research development and presentation

that student would be required to present their research, the curriculum committee recently agreed to add a Communication Studies course to the curriculum. This course requires students to prepare and deliver informative and persuasive speeches as well as evaluate the discourse of others. The committee members perceived this course would enhance students' communication and critical thinking skills and their level of confidence.

INITIAL STEPS AND A MAJOR ERROR

In the past, there were scattered opportunities through an independent study course for social work students to join with some faculty members in varied research projects. Nothing was formalized in the BSSW curriculum to assure that a research possibility would be available to all majors. The first step was to determine what type of research should be required and where in the curriculum it would be implemented.

There was agreement among the faculty that students' research should be beneficial to the community, rather than some hypothetical project. Staff and administrators of social service agencies had regularly voiced to faculty that they lacked time to conduct necessary research in areas such as: unmet community needs, effective interventions, program effectiveness, and client satisfaction. To address these agency needs, a decision was made to connect a required research project to a student's field practice site. A textbook devoted to agency-based research would be required reading for the students and would be provided to each field instructor.

Students in the BSSW program spend two full days per week for the entire academic year in a senior field placement. In addition, they are required to attend a two-hour field seminar once a week. The seminar instructor is also the field liaison for the students. At the time the research project was instituted, there were 35 seniors in field practice who were divided into three field seminar sections. The sections were taught by one full-time tenure track faculty member and two adjuncts. The research project was divided into six parts; three parts (literature review, problem identification and methodology) to be completed in fall term and three parts (data collection, analysis, interpretation and recommendations for future research) to be completed in spring term. There was an assumption that seminar leaders as well as field instructors would assist students with the suitability of proposed projects as well as mentor them as they proceeded to complete each part of the assignment. This assumption proved to be false.

Field instructors and the two adjunct instructors provided limited assistance. In some cases there appeared to be a lack of appreciation for the importance of research in social work practice and in most instances there was considerable discomfort with the assignment due to deficient research skills. Some of the field instructors voiced that the research assignment was taking too much time away from other field responsibilities. The full-time tenure track faculty member who was teaching one section of the seminar was bombarded with requests for assistance from students in all the seminar sections as well as from the adjuncts and field instructors. In less than two years, the adjuncts conducting the seminars decided to no longer teach in the program due to their anxiety with the research assignment. Something had to change.

THE ASSIGNMENT IS MOVED

A significant shift occurred in 2003-2004 when the faculty decided to move the assignment from the field seminars to two required senior-level social work courses; Social Work Practice Methods III in fall term and Integrative Seminar in spring term. Both courses were taught by full-time, tenure-track faculty who valued research and had excellent research skills. The Practice Methods III with its focus on larger social systems and the Integrative Seminar, a capstone course, were an appropriate venue for the assignment. Due to the lockstep nature of the curriculum, the seniors enrolled in Practice Methods III in fall term would be enrolled in the Integrative Seminar in spring term. The nature of the assignment itself did not change. What had changed was greater availability of research expertise and counseling as well as reinforcement in the classroom regarding the importance of research to effective practice. Field consultants no longer played a key role in the assignment.

CONNECTING TO THE EXHIBITION

In 1996, The University of Tennessee had established the Exhibition of Undergraduate Research and Creative Achievement to recognize and celebrate the original scholarly work completed each year by undergraduate students. This event recognizes the interest and scholarly work of students beyond the perimeters of the classroom as well as the faculty who mentor students and promote professional work in the discipline. The Exhibition existed prior to the formalized research effort in the BSSW program. A few students worked with faculty through an independent study course to design and implement a limited project. They entered the Exhibition with some success. As more BSSW students heard about and attended the Exhibition, interest grew. When the BSSW faculty initially decided to require all students to conduct a research project, the focus was on conducting research rather than the communication of the results beyond the field practice setting. The Exhibition of Undergraduate Research and Creative Achievement provided an additional learning opportunity for students.

Understanding the importance of presenting research, the faculty decided in 2002 to require all seniors to enter their research project with a poster presentation in the 2003 Exhibition of Undergraduate Research and Creative Achievement. At this time the project was still connected to the field seminars. This added dimension to the research project dictated that additional faculty time had to be devoted to the initiative. The professor in the Integrative Seminar worked with students to present data in poster format. A text related to the development of posters was required. A PhD student was assigned to meet with individual students as needed. Due to scheduling difficulty, few students took advantage of this resource.

When the project was moved to Practice Methods III and the Integrative Seminar, the instructors of the classes were expected to mentor the students. It became readily apparent in 2003 that the instructors were hard pressed to meet their teaching and scholarship responsibilities as well as mentor and assist students in their research projects. With support of the dean, a decision was made to assign a faculty member to work with individual students throughout the academic year. This assignment became a part of the faculty member's workload. Now students had the opportunity to meet with a faculty member on a regular basis and whenever they had questions or problems. As indicated in student evaluations of the research project, this decision has proven to be very beneficial.

IRB REVIEW

When the Exhibition of Undergraduate Research and Creative Achievement originated, there was little consideration of IRB review and approval. There was an assumption that the projects were class assignments and approval was not deemed necessary. After the BSSW program tied the research assignment into field practice and required all seniors to enter the Exhibition, the University began to look more closely at human subject clearance. There became a growing concern that sensitive information might be displayed in a public forum. At first the University's IRB Committee requested an abbreviated review that allowed the BSSW program to summarize the projects on one form. Later this requirement changed to each project had to be submitted individually on a Form A (an expedited review). This challenge provided another learning opportunity for students. Students now are taught in the practice methods course how to complete a Form A in a timely manner in order to proceed with their projects. Currently there is some discussion that a more intense review (Form B) is appropriate. The type of IRB review is still being debated.

CLEARANCE FOR AGENCY RESEARCH

When the research project became a requirement for the field seminars and later to two required courses, students had to move quickly to address the components of the assignment. Field instructors provided their support to the students' efforts, often without formal clearance from agency administration. At times problems occurred when agency administrators became aware of the research. Some administrators were weary of information regarding agency services being made public and concerned about issues of confidentiality. On a few occasions, administrators "pulled the plug" on a project even with verbal assurance from faculty that confidentiality would be maintained. Students had to scramble to find another project and to complete the assignment with less than desired results. To address any agency concern and to protect students who were engaged in a research project, the BSSW program developed an agreement that had to be signed and dated early in the academic year by the field instructor and agency administrator. The agreement identifies that the student is working on an agency-based project and the student's work will be submitted to the Exhibition of Undergraduate Research and Creative Achievement at the University of Tennessee. This form also points out that all results are submitted in aggregate form with no agency identification and all projects have been reviewed and approved by the University of Tennessee College of Social Work's Human Subjects Committee. The utilization of the form brought concerns to the forefront early in the semester. Now needed adjustments in a project can be made in a timely matter.

STUDENT SUCCESS

Since the inauguration of the Exhibition of Undergraduate Research and Creative Achievement in 1997, numerous BSSW students have received awards. Chart 2 identifies the number of students who participated in the Exhibition and the number of awards obtained for each year.

CHART 2

Year	Participants	Awards
1997	2	1
1998	3	0
1999	6	1
2000	3	0
2001	5	1
2002	4	1
2003	34	5*
2004	28	5*
2005	22	4

*one of these students also received a "Best of Show" award

In addition to awards received at the Exhibition, two student papers have been published in refereed journals and one paper in a national social work magazine.

EVALUATIONS

From 2003 to the present, members of the senior class have been requested to complete a survey that addresses the preparation that they received for the development and presentation of the senior research project. The survey also focuses on how this project assisted students in their improvement of research skills and knowledge.

In evaluating the preparation received for the research project, the seniors were asked to use a Likert-type scale (5-Excellent, 4-More than Adequate, 3-Adequate, 2-Less than Adequate, 1-Poor). As Chart 3 indicates,

CHART 3. Preparation for the Project

Item	2005 Mean Score	2004 Mean Score	2003 Mean Score
Availability of materials (poster) for the research fair	4.86	4.31	3.87
Availability of special faculty assistance	4.57	4.42	3.24
Information regarding the development of a poster board presentation	4.36	3.73	3.24
Information regarding the availability of special faculty assistance for the project	4.21	4.19	3.30
Information regarding the presentation of your data at the research fair	4.21	3.73	3.24
Assistance from your field instructor in developing your research question	4.07	3.12	2.76
Support from your field instructor in implementing the research project	4.00	3.35	3.30
Content and information from SW 412 (Practice III)	3.93	3.35	***
Content and skills taught in SW 310 (Social Work Research)	3.93	3.35	2.94
Content and information from SW 460 (Integrative Seminar)	3.78	3.31	3.18
Content from your statistics class (Psychology 385 or Math 115)	3.50	2.94	2.70
Assistance from your field liaison (seminar leader) in implementing the research project	**	**	2.73

**This item was not included in the 2005 and 2004 survey. Seminar leaders are no longer directly involved in the project.
***In 2003 the research assignment was not included in SW 412.

in 2005 the students perceived that they received "adequate" to "more then adequate" assistance in preparing for the project. In addition, the chart provides the mean scores from the 2004 and 2003 survey. A comparison of scores indicates a steady and often a substantial improvement for each item. Moving the assignment from the field seminars in 2003-2004 and providing additional faculty guidance and support appears to be paying rich dividends.

The survey also addressed how many times students met in person with a faculty member to discuss their research project and what was the average length of time for each meeting. As Chart 4 indicates, the number of visits per student and the average length of time for each visit have increased each year. It seems the seniors are taking advantage of the increased faculty assistance. Also the results point to the project as being time intensive. Keep in mind that the results reflected face to face contact and did not take into account e-mail and telephone conversations.

Using a Likert-type scale (5-Strongly Agree, 4-Agree, 3-Neutral, 2-Disagree, and 1-Strongly disagree) the seniors are requested to assess the development of their research skills and knowledge due to their involvement in this project. Chart 5 provides a comparison of mean scores for each item in 2005, 2004, and 2003. Results display an appreciable increase in agreement on all items from 2003 to 2005. It is comforting to see the importance of research in social work practice receiving a high score each year.

The seniors are asked to use a Likert-type scale (5-Extremely Confident, 4-Very Confident, 3-Confident, 2-Less Than Confident, and 1-Not Confident At All) to indicated their level of confidence in the production and presentation of research if employed by a social services agency or enrolled in a graduate social work program. As Chart 6 indicates, each year the seniors identified being more confident in an academic setting than an agency setting. The perceived availability of continued faculty assistance in the academic setting may have an influence. The scores in the level of confidence category, unlike the

CHART 4. Faculty Consultation

Year	Average Number of Visits	Length of Time (minutes)
2003	3.8	24
2004	4.69	25.58
2005	5.01	30.36

CHART 5. Development of Research Skills and Knowledge

Item	2005 Mean Score	2004 Mean Score	2003 Mean Score
The research assignment helped me to understand the importance of research in social work practice	4.71	4.04	4.09
The research project enhanced me to think critically	4.50	3.85	3.67
This project gave me confidence to conduct future research	4.43	3.88	3.67
This assignment helped me to learn how to develop a poster presentation	4.43	4.12	3.79
Conducting and presenting this research increased my interest to conduct and present research in the future	4.29	3.35	3.24
This assignment helped me learn how to select a methodology	4.29	3.77	3.36
This project helped me develop problem-solving skills	4.29	3.69	3.52
This assignment helped me learn how to conduct a literature review	4.21	3.88	3.52
I feel the research project prepared me for graduate social work education	4.21	3.69	3.73
This project made me more aware of ethical considerations in conducting research	4.14	3.65	3.58
This assignment helped me learn how to define a problem	4.00	3.96	3.39
I feel the research project prepared me for social work practice	4.07	3.54	3.55
This assignment helped me learn how to code data	4.00	3.23	3.18
This assignment helped me learn how to analyze data	3.93	3.69	3.36

other two previous categories, are rather erratic from year to year. Further evaluation needs to occur before any conclusions can be drawn.

In a series of open-ended questions the seniors are asked to identify the following: the key elements that allowed them to complete the research project; the biggest challenges in developing and implementing the project; and curricular changes to better prepare them for this assignment. Each year seniors perceived faculty mentoring as the key to completing the project. The percentage of students mentioning this factor has increased each year. A number of students have also appreciated that the project was broken down into a number of steps throughout the academic year. In 2003, the biggest challenge for students was collecting data due to limited support from their field agencies. There was a consensus that the field consultants and field supervisors should play a

CHART 6. Level of Confidence

Item	2005 Mean Score	2004 Mean Score	2003 Mean Score
You were required in a class to develop a research project	4.07	3.52	3.65
You were required to discuss the results of your research project in your class or in an agency	4.00	3.56	3.74
You saw the need for some evaluative research and would say so at an agency meeting	3.79	3.2	3.44
You were requested to report your findings in front of your agency's board of directors	3.64	3.44	3.41
You were requested by your supervisor to conduct a research project for your agency	3.64	3.22	3.31

more active role. In more recent surveys, the students' biggest challenges have been inputting and analyzing data and discussing their research at the Exhibition. Curricular changes that have been suggested have included: increased exposure and training for inputting data; greater instruction on problem identification; additional practice in making professional presentations; and further discussion regarding poster design.

Seniors in the BSSW program are requested to anonymously complete an exit survey. They are asked to use a Likert-type scale (5-Extremely Helpful, 4-Very Helpful, 3-Helpful, 2-Not Very helpful, 1-Not Helpful At All) to answer questions regarding helpfulness of the program in preparing them to meet the educational objectives. One of the program's educational objectives addresses the use of research methods to evaluate the extent to which goals of the change process have been met. The mean score for this item has improved from 3.90 in 2003 to 4.21 in 2005. Students are asked to answer open-ended questions regarding the strengths and weaknesses of the program. One of the perceived strengths regularly mentioned is the research project. An identified weakness is limited opportunities to input and analyze data.

PROGRAM RESPONSE

Outcomes procedures per se guarantee nothing by way of curricular improvement. The key is using information from these measures to improve teaching, learning, and the overall effectiveness of the program. The data collected from the Senior Research Project Survey and the

Senior Exit Survey has been influential in changing the placement of the project in the curriculum, the addition of a speech communication course to degree requirements, and the reorganization of a faculty member's workload. The social work research class has been revised to included greater opportunity for inputting and analyzing data. The Integrative Seminar has added information regarding research and poster presentations; in fact the course has a required text that is a guide to poster presentations. This course also requires each student to give an oral presentation related to the research project.

CONCLUSION

The social work profession has an ethical obligation to be equipped with scientific evidence of the highest quality when addressing human needs. The National Association of Social Workers (NASW) Code of Ethics identifies that social workers "should critical examine and keep current with emerging knowledge . . . (and) base practice on recognized knowledge, including empirically based knowledge relevant to social work and social work ethics" (4.01). The Council on Social Work Education (CSWE) is clear that future social workers need to value the importance of research to practice and be able to use research skills. CSWE (2003) clearly identifies in accreditation standard 4.6 that research content must prepare students "to develop, use, and effectively communicate empirically based knowledge, including evidence-based interventions" (p. 36).

The BSSW program at the University of Tennessee College of Social work has made a major commitment to undergraduate research. The program has infused research content throughout its curriculum. An environment has been established that fosters an appreciation and understanding of the central role of scientific findings to practice and provides learning opportunities to conduct agency-based research. Since 1999, the program has come to realize that a research initiative requires a strong, continuous commitment from faculty and administration; mentoring of students by full-time faculty who have excellent research skills; ongoing assessment; curricular adjustments based on assessments; and flexibility in dealing with agencies and human subjects committees.

The author understands that every undergraduate social work program is unique. Programs must make their own decisions regarding how to prepare their students for the needed research competencies for effective practice in the contemporary world, as well as how to meet

CSWE's expectations for research content and skill development. It is the author's intent that this descriptive paper will provide some ideas for discussion and further thinking about preparing undergraduate social work students to passionately seek evidence of effectiveness in their helping services.

REFERENCES

Boyer Commission on Educating Undergraduates in the Research University. (1998). *Reinventing undergraduate education: A blueprint for America's research universities*. Stony Brook, NY: State University of New York at Stony Brook for the Carnegie Foundation for the Advancement of Teaching.

Collins, J. & Porras, J. I. (1997). *Built to last: Successful habits of visionary companies*. New York: HarperCollins Publishers, Inc.

Council on Social Work Education-Commission on Accreditation (2003). *Handbook of accreditation standards and procedures*, 5th Edition. Alexandria, VA: Council on Social Work Education.

National Association of Social Worker. (1999). *Code of ethics of the National Association of Social Workers*. Washington, DC: National Association of Social Workers.

doi:10.1300/J394v04n01_02

Sexually Abused Children: Symptomatology and Incidence of Problematic Sexual Behaviors

Kristina M. Kulesz
Wendy J. Wyse

SUMMARY. The effect of sexual abuse on children has been found to be highly variable. This study examines the symptomatology of 100 children who have been sexually abused, including the incidence of problematic sexual behaviors. Emotional and behavioral symptoms were measured using two symptom scales: internalizing and externalizing. Results revealed that younger children experienced significantly more internalizing and externalizing symptoms as compared with older children. Thirty percent of the sample did exhibit problematic sexual behaviors, and all of these children were under the age of 13. Finally, children who did exhibit problematic sexual behaviors scored significantly higher on both the internalizing and externalizing symptom scales as compared with children who did not exhibit these behaviors. These findings suggest that young children who display sexual behavior problems are not only the most symptomatic of the sexually abused, but may be at significant risk of becoming sexual offenders themselves. Early identification and effective treatment of these victims may prevent the victimization of

Kristina M. Kulesz and Wendy J. Wyse are affiliated with The University of Tennessee, 303 Henson Hall, Knoxville, TN 37996 (E-mail: wwyse@utk.edu).

[Haworth co-indexing entry note]: "Sexually Abused Children: Symptomatology and Incidence of Problematic Sexual Behaviors." Kulesz, Kristina M., and Wendy J. Wyse. Co-published simultaneously in *Journal of Evidence-Based Social Work* (The Haworth Press, Inc.) Vol. 4, No. 1/2, 2007, pp. 27-46; and: *Building Excellence: The Rewards and Challenges of Integrating Research into the Undergraduate Curriculum* (ed: Catherine N. Dulmus, and Karen M. Sowers) The Haworth Press, 2007, pp. 27-46. Single or multiple copies of this article are available for a fee from The Haworth Document Delivery Service [1-800-HAWORTH, 9:00 a.m. - 5:00 p.m. (EST). E-mail address: docdelivery@haworthpress.com].

other children, perhaps interrupting the cycle of sexual abuse. doi: 10.1300/ J394v04n01_03 *[Article copies available for a fee from The Haworth Document Delivery Service: 1-800-HAWORTH. E-mail address: <docdelivery@haworth press.com> Website: <http://www.HaworthPress.com> © 2007 by The Haworth Press, Inc. All rights reserved.]*

KEYWORDS. Sexual abuse, children, internalizing behaviors, externalizing behaviors, sexual behaviors

INTRODUCTION

Child sexual abuse has been established as a serious international problem. For the past twenty years, many studies have sought to illuminate this problem and to explain or predict the presence of different symptoms associated with child sexual abuse. Finkelhor (1994) examined studies on child sexual abuse conducted in 19 different nations and found abuse rates ranging from 7% to 36% for women and 3% to 29% for men, similar to North American rates. In a recent meta-analysis, the prevalence of child sexual abuse in the United States was estimated to be a staggering 30-40% of female children and 13% of male children (Bolen, 2001). In a ten-year research review, Putnam (2003) summarized demographic risk factors for child sexual abuse and found that being a female, being older in age, being disabled, or having an absent parent are positive risk factors for child sexual abuse, while socioeconomic status and race or ethnicity were not significant risk factors.

Studies of school-based samples of adolescents have revealed interesting data regarding the incidence of child sexual abuse and of sexually aggressive behaviors. Lodico (1996) found a sexual abuse prevalence rate of 10% in a large sample of ninth and twelfth grade adolescents in a Midwestern state, with minority students and females experiencing a greater likelihood of having been sexually abused. Of those who did report a childhood history of sexual abuse, they were also six times more likely to be at risk for sexual coercion (reported as either forcing someone else into sexual contact or being forced into sexual contact; Lodico, 1996).

In a similar study, Borowsky, Hogan and Ireland (1997) examined another large sample of ninth and twelfth grade Midwestern adolescents and found that 4.8% of males and 1.3% of females reported forcing someone into a sexual act. Risk factors for these sexually aggressive adolescents included having been sexually or physically abused, having witnessed abuse involving other family members, and alcohol or drug problems among family members (Borowsky et al., 1997).

Given the astounding estimates of the prevalence of sexual abuse worldwide and the possibility that victims of sexual abuse may, in turn, become sexually aggressive toward other children, it is important to identify those who are at risk of exhibiting problematic sexually behaviors. This study seeks to better understand the symptomatology of children who have been sexually abused, including the incidence of problematic sexual behaviors, so these children can receive early intervention in the clinical setting.

Symptomotology of the Sexually Abused Child

The effect of sexual abuse on children is highly variable. In a synthesis of 45 studies, Kendall-Tackett, Williams, and Finkelhor (1993) found a range of 12 symptom groups present in children who were sexually abused including symptoms of anxiety, fear, Post-Traumatic Stress Disorder (PTSD), depression, poor self-esteem, somatic complaints, mental illness, aggression, sexualized behaviors, school/learning problems, behavior problems, and self-destructive behaviors. They also reported between 21-49% of children in the studies reviewed were asymptomatic. The authors found that sexualized behaviors and PTSD were the two symptoms most consistently exhibited by child sexual abuse victims. Studies reviewed had rates of inappropriate sexual behavior ranging from 35% for preschool age children to 24% for mixed age children (Kendall-Tackett et al., 1993). Interestingly, school age children and adolescents had significantly lower rates of inappropriate sexual behaviors (6% and 0%, respectively; Kendall-Tackett et al., 1993). Putnam (2003) also found that sexualized behaviors in children were the most commonly documented outcome in a ten-year literature review.

Besides sexualized behaviors, children who are sexually abused also commonly exhibit other behaviors. Early work regarding children's emotional and behavioral problems revealed two major groupings of behaviors. Though recently these two groupings have been more commonly referred to as internalizing and externalizing behaviors, other studies have referred to them as overcontrolled and undercontrolled or personality disorder and conduct disorder (Achenbach, 1985; Edelbrock, 1979; Quay, 1986). The internalizing grouping is often characterized by feelings of inferiority, self-consciousness, shyness, anxiety, crying, social withdrawal, hypersensitivity or depression (Achenbach, 1985; Edelbrock, 1979; Quay, 1986). The externalizing grouping is commonly characterized by aggression, disobedience, disruptiveness, fighting, temper tantrums, defiance, irritability or quarrelsomeness (Achenbach, 1985; Edelbrock, 1979; Quay, 1986). Recent studies have found high comorbidity between internalizing and externalizing problems (McConaugh & Skiba, 1993).

Gale, Thompson, Moran, and Sack (1988) found high rates of symptomatology among a clinical population of children who were sexually abused. Ninety-five percent of the children displayed at least one symptom, while 61% of them displayed at least three symptoms. Specifically, Gale and colleagues (1988) found a range of symptoms including fears, nightmares, clinging, sadness, withdrawal, anxiety and aggression among this sample.

Hazzard, Celano, Gould, Lawry, and Webb (1995) examined symptomatology of a predominately African American, low-income sample of girls aged 8 to 13 who were sexually abused using many different measures. Caretakers completed measures on the amount of abuse related support the child was receiving, caretaker attributions, and the child's internalizing and externalizing symptoms. Children completed measures on their attributional style and PTSD symtomatology. The researchers found that characteristics of the abuse incident were not related to symptomatology. They did, however, find a significant positive relationship between the child's relationship with the perpetrator and the child's overall adjustment as assessed by a clinician. Likewise, girls who had a supportive relationship with their caretaker were rated by their caretakers as exhibiting less internalizing and externalizing symptoms (Hazzard et al., 1995).

Another study examined the differences in trauma symptoms experienced by a sample of adolescents who were sexually abused and who voluntarily referred for counseling services. Researchers found 53% of the sample experienced clinically significant symptoms as measured by the Trauma Symptom Checklist for Children and the Clinician-Administered PTSD Scale for Children and Adolescents (Bal, De Bourdeaudhuij, Crombez, & Van Oost, 2004). These authors also found no significant symptom differences between adolescents who were victims of intra- or extra-familial abuse.

Other studies have found contradictory results regarding whether characteristics of the abuser or the abuse incident affect the symptoms experienced by victims. Sexually abused girls, a psychiatric control group of girls, and a nonpsychiatric control group of girls, age 6 to 12, were compared with regard to sexualized behaviors and psychopathology (Consentino, Meyer-Bahlburg, Alpert, Weinberg, & Gaines, 1995). Both sexually abused girls and psychiatric controls exhibited more internalizing and externalizing behaviors compared with non-psychiatric controls. Sexually abused girls showed more sexual behavior problems than either of the other two groups. In addition, abuse by fathers or stepfathers that involved intercourse was associated with marked sexual behavior problems for a small subset of sexually abused girls (Cosentino et al., 1995).

Several studies have examined the incidence or characteristics of children with problematic sexual behaviors or children who have molested other children. Gale and colleagues (1988) found that 41% of the children in their sample who were victims of sexual abuse exhibited inappropriate sexual behavior as compared with only 4% of children who were physically abused and 3% of children who were not abused. According to another study, nearly 40% of the abuse to children with sexual behavior problems was performed by other children or adolescents (Gray, Busconi, Houchens, & Pithers, 1997). In a study of 13 girls who had molested other girls, Johnson (1989) found that 100% of them had been victims of sexual abuse. And finally, in a sample of incarcerated adolescent male sexual offenders, "45% of the sample admitted to sexual offending prior to age 12 and 47% reported having been children with sexual behavior problems" (Burton, 2000, p. 44). Offenders who began abusing before age 12 were more likely to have committed penetration acts only (Burton, 2000). Friedrich and Luecke (1988) studied a small group of sexually aggressive children and an equal-sized group of boys who completed a sexual abuse treatment program. Eighty-one percent of the sexually aggressive group had been sexually abused, with 100% of these children having experienced oral/anal or vaginal intercourse with adult perpetrators.

Other studies have found conflicting results concerning the percentage of sexually aggressive children who were sexually abused. Fago (2003), in a sample of predominantly male subjects referred for sexually aggressive behavior, found that 72% reported they had not experienced previous physical or sexual abuse and only 18% of the sample had been sexually abused. Therefore, it is important to recognize that not all children who exhibit sexually aggressive behaviors were victims of sexual abuse. However, there appears to be a fairly high percentage of children who do act out sexually after having been sexually abuse. It appears this is especially true for young girls.

Children with problematic sexual behaviors are a particularly vulnerable population who are also at high risk for other psychiatric or behavioral problems. One study found that 100% of a small sample of sexually aggressive children were also diagnosed with a psychiatric disorder such as conduct disorder, oppositional defiant disorder, schizophrenia, adjustment disorder or dysthymia (Friedrich & Luecke, 1988). Gray and colleagues (1997) found that 93% of their sample met the diagnostic criteria for at least one psychiatric disorder. Seventy-one percent of these children exhibited clinically significant internalizing behaviors and 76% exhibited clinically significant externalizing behaviors as measured by the Child Behavior Checklist (Gray et al., 1997). Finally, another study of children who were sexually aggressive found that a high proportion of the children were diagnosed with Attention Deficit/ Hyperactivity Disorder and Conduct Disorders (Pithers, Gray, Busconi, & Houchens, 1998). Despite this information, there is still debate regarding whether children who exhibit problematic sexual behaviors are, in fact, more symptomatic than other children who have been sexually abused but do not exhibit such behaviors.

Continuum of Problematic Sexual Behaviors

The sexual behaviors of children fall along a continuum from age-appropriate sexual behavior to problematic sexual behaviors including the sexual molestation of other children (Johnson, 1993). Problematic sexual behaviors may be defined as any sexual behaviors exhibited by children that are not normal sexual exploration. Johnson (1993) defines normal sexual exploration as a voluntary information gathering process whereby children of similar age and size explore each other's bodies visually and tactilely or try out gender roles or behaviors.

According to Johnson (1993), problematic sexual behaviors may be categorized under one of three groups: sexually reactive behaviors, extensive mutual sexual behaviors, or children who molest other children. Sexually reactive children display more sexualized behaviors than their peers and their focus on sexuality may result from exposure to pornography or other age-inappropriate sexual explicit stimuli. Generally, children who are sexually reactive engage in sexual behaviors that involve their own bodies such as excessive masturbation, exposing their genitals or inserting objects in themselves but do not engage in the coercion or victimization of other children for sexual purposes (Johnson, 1993). Sexually reactive children have not necessarily been sexually abused and some may have only been inappropriately exposed to sexualized stimuli.

The concept of sexual reactivity has been defined differently in the literature. Friedrich (1990) defines sexual reactivity in children as those sexualized behaviors that seem to be the direct reaction to recent sexual abuse. According to Friedrich, sexual reactivity may simply be a heightened sexuality or may involve actual sexual aggression toward other children (Friedrich, 1990). Clearly, according to this definition, sexually reactive children have indeed been sexually abused in some manner.

According to Johnson (1993), the second group of problematic sexual behaviors involves extensive mutual sexual behaviors. Johnson (1993) characterizes this group as children who participate in the full spectrum of adult sexual behaviors (oral copulation, vaginal and anal intercourse, etc) with children of similar age. While these children may use persuasion to get other children to engage in sexual acts with them, they usually do not use force or emotional coercion (Johnson, 1993).

Finally, children who molest other children also engage in the full spectrum of adult sexual behaviors, but also typically force penetration of the vagina or anus of another child with objects and use emotionally coercion. Sexualized behaviors in this group of children are characterized by impulsivity, compulsivity and aggression (Johnson, 1993). These children are also commonly referred to as sexually aggressive children.

Other researchers have grouped children with sexual behavior problems using empirical methods. Pithers, Gray, Busconi, and Houchens (1998) used cluster analyses to identify five subtypes of children with sexual behavior problems. The five subtypes (Nondisordered, Abuse Reactive, Highly Traumatized, Rule Breakers, and Sexually Aggressive children) were found to differ in psychiatric diagnosis, maltreatment history, age of onset of problematic sexual behaviors, performance of highly aggressive sexually abusive behaviors, and the tendency to engage in nonsexual acting out. Based on the results, Sexually Aggressive and Rule Breaker subtypes were at the highest risk for engaging in delinquent and criminal behavior. Overrepresented by males, the Sexual Aggressive group was most likely to commit a penetrative sexual act whereas females were overrepresented in the Rule Breaker group and scored significantly higher on the Child Behavior Checklist Sex Problems scale as compared with all other groups.

Certainly, not every child who has been sexually abused will exhibit problematic sexual behaviors. But for those who do, it appears as if children who exhibit problematic sexual behaviors at a young age and continue through adolescence are most at risk of serious psychopathology and of becoming sexual offenders. It is therefore important to identify child victims who do exhibit problematic sexual behaviors as early as possible so that prevention and intervention efforts may be appropriately directed. Other children may experience emotional and behavioral symptoms as a result of the abuse that are not sexual in nature, while still other children may be completely asymptomatic. A clearer understanding of all of these groups of children would benefit clinicians who treat children who have been sexually abused.

Therefore, this study seeks to understand the presenting symptomatology of a clinical sample of children who have been sexually abused, including the incidence of problematic sexual behaviors. This sample of sexually abused children will be described using the dimensions of internalizing and externalizing symptoms. The following research questions will be answered in this study: Do children who have been sexually abused experience symptoms differently according to their age or gender? What is the incidence of problematic sexual behaviors among this sample of children? Are children who display problematic sexual behaviors more likely to experience internalizing and externalizing symptoms when compared with children who do not display problematic sexual behaviors? Does a child's gender or age affect the likelihood that the child will experience symptoms, especially if they do exhibit problematic sexual behaviors?

METHOD

Sample

One hundred children who received clinical services at a southeastern sexual assault counseling center were selected for this study. Subjects were selected from the center's intake log book by systematic random sampling where every fifth child was selected for participation. All subjects were victims of child sexual abuse and had completed an intake at the agency within a three year time frame (January 2000-December 2002). Victims were referred to the center by state agency personnel, school personnel, mental health and medical professionals, or by self-referral. This study was approved by the University of Tennessee Institutional Review Board. The majority of the sample was female (N = 72) and under the age of thirteen (N = 80). Ninety-six percent of the subjects were Caucasian, 3% were African American, and 1% were Hispanic.

Data Collection

Each child victim and his or her primary caregiver participated in a semi-structured clinical interview facilitated by a trained therapist or supervised intern at the first appointment at the sexual assault agency. During this intake appointment, a thorough psychosocial assessment was completed based on information provided by both the primary caregiver and the child. At the time of intake, all children were identified as victims of sexual abuse as reported by the child or family member and all were under the age of eighteen.

Systematic record reviews were conducted for each subject selected for inclusion in this study by a trained researcher. Data regarding demographics, recent emotional and behavioral functioning, and any information regarding problematic sexual behaviors was collected on a data collection sheet (Appendix) developed for the purposes of this study. The data collection sheet did not include any identifying client information.

Measurement

Demographic characteristics. The victim's gender was recorded as male or female. Age of the victim at the time of the incident was dichotomized as 13 to 17 years of age and under age 13. Ethnicity of the victim was categorized as European American (Caucasian), African American, Hispanic, Asian or Pacific Islander, American Indian, or other. Of the one hundred children sampled in this study, 72% (N = 72) were female, 96% (N = 96) were Caucasian, and 80% (N = 80) were under the age of thirteen. Because of the relative homogeneous ethnic make-up of this sample, ethnicity was excluded from future data analyses.

Problematic sexual behaviors. Problematic sexual behaviors are defined as any sexual behaviors exhibited by children that are not normal sexual exploration. Johnson (1993) defines normal sexual exploration as a voluntary information gathering process whereby children of similar age and size explore each other's bodies visually and tactilely or try out gender roles or behaviors. This definition includes all three of the levels of problematic sexual behaviors as described by Johnson (1993) in the continuum of problematic sexual behaviors. Therefore, identification of any one of the following behaviors resulted in a positive response on the data collection sheet as evidence of a problematic sexual behavior: demonstration of sexualized activities, knowledge, gestures, and language deemed developmentally inappropriate; excessive masturbation; preoccupation with sexual ideas and activities; interest in or attempt of sexual contact with older children, adolescents, adults, or animals; engagement in or attempt of sexual encounters with same age or younger children (including masturbation, oral sex, digital penetration, and intercourse); or sexual molestation other children.

Symptomatology. Data were collected on the presence or absence of 46 different indicators of problematic emotional or behavioral functioning within 3 months of the child's victimization as reported by the victim or the victim's caregiver. Frequency distributions for these indicators were examined first and those variables with a very low base rate (5% or less) were eliminated from the study. Based on this criterion, seven indicators were removed from the study leaving 39 indicators. Two indicators were eliminated because they are included under the definition of problematic sexual behaviors (excessive masturbation and sexual acting out).

In order to operationalize the symptoms experienced by this clinical sample of children, the remaining 37 indicators of emotional and behavioral functioning were then grouped into internalizing and externalizing behaviors according to McConaughy and Skiba (1993) and two symptom scales were developed. For the purposes of this study, internalizing symptoms included emotions and behaviors indicative of anxiety, depression, somatic complaints and withdrawal (McConaughy & Skiba, 1993). Externalizing symptoms included emotions and behaviors indicative of aggressive and delinquent behavior, attention problems and hyperactivity (McConaughy & Skiba, 1993). The two scales were developed and the internal consistency reliability of the two sets of items was examined. Items with corrected item-total correlations less than .30 were deleted (six items from the internalizing scale and two items from the externalizing scale). This resulted in a set of 12 items for the internalizing scale ($\alpha = .80$) and 17 items for the externalizing scale ($\alpha = .86$). The correlation between these two scales was .34 ($p < .001$). Scores on both scales were normally distributed. Univariate and bivariate analyses were conducted in order to answer the research questions presented.

RESULTS

Using the internalizing and externalizing symptom scales developed for this study, the following research questions were addressed: (a) Do children who have been sexually abused experience symptoms differently according to their age or gender? (b) What is the incidence of problematic sexual behaviors among this sample of children? (c) Are children who display problematic sexual behaviors more likely to experience internalizing or externalizing symptoms than children who do not display problematic sexual behaviors? (d) Does a child's gender or age affect the likelihood that the child will experience internalizing and externalizing symptoms, especially if they do exhibit problematic sexual behaviors?

Univariate analyses were first conducted to determine the frequency with which internalizing and externalizing symptoms were experienced by the sample. Looking at both the internalizing and externalizing symptom scales combined, 91% (N = 91) of the sample reported at least one symptom with an average of 7.12 symptoms per person (*SD* = 6.50), leaving only 9% of the sample asymptomatic. Only 17% of the sample was asymptomatic on the internalizing scale and 24% of the sample was asymptomatic on the externalizing scale. The mean number of internalizing symptoms reported was 3.19 and the mean number of externalizing symptoms was 3.93 (*SD* = 2.86 and 3.78, respectively). When the frequency distributions of the internalizing and externalizing scales were analyzed, 64% of the sample exhibited at least three internalizing symptoms and 56% exhibited at least three externalizing symptoms.

Our first research question concerned the relationship between internalizing and externalizing symptoms and the gender or age of the child. A series of t-tests were conducted to test whether the mean scores on the internalizing and externalizing scales varied with the age or gender of the child. Table 1 summarizes the results of comparisons on the two scales by the child's age and Table 2 summarizes the results of comparisons on the two scales by gender. Mean scores on the internalizing scale were higher for males than females, but the difference was not statistically

TABLE 1. Mean Scores on Symptom Scale by Age

Scale	Younger	Older
Internalizing	3.64	1.40
	(2.97)	(1.35)
Externalizing	4.34	2.30
	(3.84)	(2.11)
N	80	20

Note. Standard deviations in parentheses.

TABLE 2. Mean Scores on Symptom Scale by Gender

Scale	Males	Females
Internalizing	4.04	2.86
	(3.40)	(2.57)
Externalizing	4.43	3.74
	(3.94)	(3.72)
N	28	72

Note. Standard deviations in parentheses.

significant ($t(98) = -1.87, p = .065$, two-tailed, $CI = -2.42$ to $.08, r_{pb} = .19$). Mean scores on the externalizing scale were also higher for males than females, but the difference was also not statistically significant ($t(98) = -.82, p = .413$, two-tailed, $CI = -2.36$ to $.98, r_{pb} = .08$). Results did, however, indicate that the mean scores on the internalizing scale were higher for younger children than older children and the difference was statistically significant ($t(98) = 3.28, p = .001$, two-tailed, $CI = .88$ to $3.59, r_{pb} = -.31$). Likewise, mean scores on the externalizing scale were also higher for younger children than older children and this difference was also statistically significant ($t(98) = 2.20, p = .030$, two-tailed, $CI = .20$ to $3.88, r_{pb} = -.22$).

The second research question was answered by examining the frequency distribution of the problematic sexual behavior variable. Univariate analyses revealed that 30% of the sample (N = 30) did exhibit problematic sexual behaviors. Of these children, 70% (N = 21) were female, 100% (N = 30) were Caucasian, and 100% (N = 30) were under the age of twelve.

To address the third and fourth research question, the sub-sample of children (N = 30) who did display sexually problematic behaviors was compared with the children who did not (N = 70). Results are summarized in Table 3. The mean internalizing score was higher for the children who did exhibit sexually problematic behaviors than the children who did not exhibit sexually problematic behaviors and this difference was statistically significant ($t(98) = -2.087, p = .005$, two-tailed, 95% $CI = -2.93$ to $-5.32, r_{pb} = .28$). Likewise, the mean externalizing score was higher for children who did exhibit problematic sexual behaviors than for children who did not exhibit these behaviors and this difference

TABLE 3. Mean Scores on Symptom Scale Compared by Problematic Sexual Behaviors

Scale	Problematic Sexual Behaviors	
	Yes	No
Internalizing	4.40	2.67
	(3.44)	(2.42)
Externalizing	5.20	3.39
	(4.36)	(3.39)
N	30	70

Note. Standard deviations in parentheses.

was also statistically significant ($t(98) = -2.246$, $p = .027$, two-tailed, 95% $CI = -3.42$ to -2.11, $r_{pb} = .22$).

Finally, the effect of gender on the likelihood of a child exhibiting problematic sexual behaviors was analyzed. Results revealed that males and females did not differ in their likelihood to exhibit problematic sexual behaviors (32.1% vs. 29.2%, X^2 (1, N = 100) = .09, $p = .771$, two-tailed, $\varphi = .03$). Age was not included in the analyses since all of the children were under the age of thirteen.

DISCUSSION

This study utilized emotional and behavioral symptom data collected from intake interviews of a clinical sample of children who were sexually abused. Internalizing and externalizing symptoms scales were developed in accordance with the literature to manage these data. Based on these scales, we first sought to evaluate whether the age or gender of the child influenced mean scores on the internalizing and externalizing symptom scales. Of this sample of 100 children who were referred to a sexual assault counseling agency, 91% of the children were experiencing at least one symptom on the internalizing and externalizing scales upon intake to the agency. Additionally, 64% of our sample exhibited at least three internalizing symptoms and 56% exhibited at least three externalizing symptoms. Finally, younger children experienced higher mean scores on both the internalizing and externalizing symptom scales than older children, while gender was not a significant factor. It is important to note that since there was no comparison group of non-abused children in this study, it is not possible to determine whether the scores on the two scales are higher or lower than scores for non-abused children.

It appears that the child's age at assessment is an important factor when examining the symptomatology of children who have been sexually abused. Portions of our findings appear consistent with studies in the literature, while other portions appear inconsistent. But these differences can likely be accounted for by closely examining the ages of the children studied. For example, consistent with our findings, Gale and colleagues (1988) found that 95% of their sample of sexually abused children who were younger than seven years old experienced at least one symptom, with 61% of the sample displaying at least three symptoms. However, the rate of asymptomatic children in the current study was much lower than other studies reported that examined samples of older children or mixed ages of children. In their synthesis, Kendall-Tackett and others (1993) found between 21-49% of children in the studies reviewed were asymptomatic. Like the sample in the current study, the studies included in this synthesis were primarily clinical samples from sexual abuse evaluation or treatment programs but the ages of the children in these studies varied. Another study found the asymptomatic rate for older children (age 12 to 18) to be 30% upon initial assessment in a clinical setting (Bal et al., 2004). Since 80% of the children in our study were under the age of 13, it appears as if the findings of this study do in fact support the contention that younger children are more symptomatic than older children. Future studies should incorporate equal portions of both age groups in the sample in order to confirm this supposition in direct comparisons.

The finding that gender was not statistically related to symptomatology is also consistent with findings in the literature. This may suggest that boys and girls who are sexually abused are likely to experience symptoms related to the abuse in a similar way and that gender does not determine how a child is affected by the abuse. In the literature, characteristics of the abuse incident(s) that include penetration, force, long duration, and high frequency, close relationship to the perpetrator, and negative relationship with non-abusing caretaker have been found to be positively related to symptomatology (Gale et al., 1988; Hazzard et al., 1995; Kendall-Tackett, 1993). Future studies should examine these factors related to the experience of symptomatology in addition to the age of the child.

Next, this study sought to determine the incidence of problematic sexual behaviors among this sample of children who had been sexually abused. Results indicated that 30% of the sample exhibited problematic sexual behaviors upon intake at the agency. This is a slightly lower rate, but comparable with other studies. Gale and colleagues (1988) found that 41% of their clinical sample exhibited inappropriate sexual behavior. Likewise, in a synthesis of several studies, rates of inappropriate sexual behavior ranged from 35% for preschool age children to 24% for mixed age children (Kendall-Tackett et al., 1993). Interestingly, school age children and adolescents had a significantly lower rate of inappropriate sexual behaviors as compared with younger children (6% and 0%, respectively; Kendall-Tackett et al., 1993). Consistent with these studies, our study found that younger children were significantly more likely to exhibit problematic sexual behaviors (Gray et al., 1997; Putnam, 2003).

In contrast with other studies, however, results of this study revealed that 70% of the children who exhibited sexually problematic behaviors were female. Friedrich and Luecke (1988) studied a small sample of children who were "sexually aggressive" (not all of the children had been sexually abused) and found that 75% of them were male. Gray and colleagues (1997) also found more males than females (65% versus 35%, respectively) in their sample of children with sexual behavior problems. Several studies have found that 100% of the girls who exhibit sexual behavior problems were victims of sexual abuse (Friedrich & Luecke, 1988; Gray et al., 1997; Johnson, 1989). Whereas, Fago (2003) found that only 18% of his predominantly male sample referred for sexually aggressive behavior had been sexually abused. Hence, since girls are 2-3 times more likely to be the victims of sexual abuse during childhood (Bolen, 2001) and males are more likely to exhibit sexual behavior problems without having been sexually abused (Fago, 2003), the restricted inclusion of only victims of sexual abuse in the current study may have affected the results of this study and may account for higher percentage of females in our sample of children with problematic sexual behaviors.

Another explanation for differences in the gender make-up of our group of children with problematic sexual behaviors may be found in the definition we used for problematic sexual behaviors. We chose to use a broad definition of problematic sexual behaviors, which encompassed all three levels of sexualized behaviors as defined by Johnson (1993). This broad definition masks the precise behaviors exhibited by the children. Future studies may want to examine each of the three categories of problematic sexual behaviors individually, comparing each of these categories with gender to detect any differences. Since many studies have found that males exhibit more sexually aggressive behaviors, it is especially important to closely examine how these sexual behaviors are defined before exact comparisons are made.

Finally, the third and fourth research questions sought to determine whether children who exhibited problematic sexual behaviors were more likely to experience internalizing or externalizing symptoms and also whether there were any gender differences for this group. For our sample, there was a significant difference between the mean scores on the internalizing and externalizing symptom scales for the children who did exhibit problematic sexual behaviors as compared with the children who did not exhibit problematic sexual behaviors. In other words, children with problematic sexual behaviors experienced more symptoms on both of the symptom scales. There was also a significant positive relationship between the overall number of symptoms reported at intake and the presence of problematic sexual behaviors.

Consistent with Consentino and others (1995), these data seem to indicate that children who are exhibiting problematic sexual behaviors are the most symptomatic overall. Gray and others (1997) found that 6-9 year old children who were exhibiting problematic sexual behaviors had higher scores on measures of symptomatology. Additionally, these children are at very high risk for other psychopathology and for eventual sexually aggression and even molestation of other children. These results are consistent with other studies that have shown children with problematic sexual behaviors are likely to meet the criteria for other psychiatric diagnoses such as Conduct Disorder, Attention Deficit/Hyperactivity Disorder, Oppositional Defiant Disorder, or Post Traumatic Stress Disorder (Cosentino et al., 1995; Friedrich & Luecke, 1988; Gale et al., 1988; Gray et al., 1997). Burton (2000) found that nearly half of his sample of incarcerated male sexual offenders exhibited sexual behavior problems before the age of 12. Since 100% of our sample was under the age of 12 and exhibiting problematic sexual behaviors, this is further evidence that these children may be particularly at risk of future sexual offenses.

This study does have some important limitations to consider. First, this study relied primarily on self-report information as provided by the caretaker and victim of sexual abuse upon intake to a treatment facility. Although the data collection instrument developed for this study did not undergo any reliability analyses, the internal consistency of the two scales was examined and did show good reliability. Future studies would be strengthened with the addition of standardized measures of child psychopathology that have been determined reliable and valid for sexually abused children, as well as incorporating other sources of information regarding the symptoms experienced by the child such as teachers.

This study did not include specific information about the nature and extent of the abuse suffered, the frequency of the abuse, or the relationship of the victim to the perpetrator. Certain studies did find that a close relationship to the perpetrator was predictive of the sexual behavior problems exhibited by the victim including molestation of other children (Consentino et al., 1995; Johnson, 1989). However, other studies have found no relationship between characteristics of the abuse incident or the relationship to the perpetrator when examining symptoms the victims reported (Bal et al., 2004; Hazzard et al., 1995). Despite this conflicting information, Kendall-Tackett, and others (1993) found in their synthesis of 45 studies that patterns of problematic sexual behaviors were likely to be different based on the age of onset of the abuse, the age of the child, the gender of the child, and the relationship to the perpetrator. Therefore, this information should be included in future studies.

Another limitation of this study is that descriptive information was not collected regarding the specific problematic sexual behaviors exhibited. Johnson (1993) discusses the importance of categorizing problematic sexual behaviors under one of three categories and cautions against treating all children as sexually aggressive children when they have not exhibited these behaviors. As discussed previously, future studies may include specific information about the sexual behaviors exhibited so that further differences between these sub-groups of children can be clarified.

In conclusion, children who have been sexually abused experience a wide range of internalizing and externalizing problems. However, given the oft reported correlation between internalizing and externalizing problems (McConaughy & Skiba, 1993), it may be helpful to evaluate whether the overall quantity of symptoms experienced by the child may also serve as an effective predictor of children who are at the highest psychological risk. Regardless of how symptoms are measured, children who exhibit problematic sexual behaviors at a young age are one group of children who need to special attention in the clinical setting. Clinicians should be especially mindful that children who display sexual behavior problems are not only the most symptomatic of the sexually abused, but are at significant risk to become sexual offenders themselves (Burton, 2000). Because approximately 40% of abuse performed by children with sexual behavior problems is performed by other children and adolescents (Gray et al., 1997), early identification and effective treatment of these young victims may prevent the victimization of other children, perhaps interrupting the cycle of sexual abuse.

REFERENCES

Achenbach, T.M. (1985). *Assessment and taxonomy of child and adolescent psychopathology.* Beverly Hills, CA: Sage.

Bal, S., De Bourdeaudhuij, I., Crombez, G., & Van Oost, P. (2004). Differences in trauma symptoms and family functioning in intra- and extrafamilial sexually abused adolescents. *Journal of Interpersonal Violence, 19*(1), 108-123.

Bolen, R.M. (2001). *Child sexual abuse: It's scope and our failure.* New York: Kluwer Academic/Plenum Publishers.

Borowsky, I.W., Hogan, M., & Ireland, M. (1997). Adolescent sexual aggression: Risk and protective factors. *Pediatrics, 100,* 7-14.

Burton, D.L. (2000). Were adolescent sexual offenders children with sexual behavior problems? *Sexual Abuse: A Journal of Research and Treatment, 12*(1), 37-48.

Cosentino, C.E., Meyer-Bahlburg, H.F.L., Alpert, J.L., Weinberg, S.L., & Ganes, R. (1995). Sexual behavior problems and psychopathology symptoms in sexually abused girls. *Journal of the American Academy of Child and Adolescent Psychiatry, 34*(8), 1033-1041.

Edelbrock, C. (1979). Empirical classification of children's behavior disorders: Progress based on parent and teacher ratings. *School Psychology Digest, 8*(4), 355-369.

Fago, D.P. (2003). Evaluation and treatment of neurodevelopmental deficits in sexually aggressive children and adolescents. *Professional Psychology: Research and Practice, 34*(3), 248-257.

Finkelhor, D. (1994). The international epidemiology of child sexual abuse. *Child Abuse & Neglect, 18*(5), 409-417.

Friedrich, W.N. (1990). *Psychotherapy of sexually abused children and their families.* New York: W.W. Norton & Company.

Friedrich, W.N., & Luecke, W.J. (1988). Young school-age sexually aggressive children. *Professional Psychology: Research and Practice, 19*(2), 155-164.

Gale, J., Thompson, R.J., Moran, T., & Sack, W.H. (1988). Sexual abuse in young children: Its clinical presentation and characteristic patterns. *Child Abuse & Neglect, 12,* 163-170.

Gray, A., Busconi, A., Houchens, P., & Pithers, W.D. (1997). Children with sexual behavior problems and their caregivers: Demographics, functioning, and clinical patterns. *Sexual Abuse: A Journal of Research and Treatment, 9*(4), 267-290.

Hazzard, A., Celano, M., Gould, J., Lawry, S., & Webb, C. (1995). Predicting symptomatology and self-blame among child sex abuse victims. *Child Abuse & Neglect, 19*(6), 707-714.

Johnson, T.C. (1989). Female Child Perpetrators: Children Who Molest Other Children. *Child Abuse & Neglect, 13,* 571-585.

Johnson, T.C. (1993). Sexual behaviors: A continuum. In E. Gil & T.C. Johnson (Eds.), *Sexualized children: Assessment and treatment of sexualized children and children who molest.* Rockville, MD: Launch Press.

Kendall-Tackett, K.A., Williams, L.M., & Finkelhor, D. (1993). Impact of sexual abuse on children: A review and synthesis of recent empirical studies. *Psychological Bulletin, 113*(1), 164-180.

Lodico, M.A., Gruber, E., & DiClemente, R.J. (1996). Childhood sexual abuse and coercive sex among school-based adolescents in a midwestern state. *Journal of Adolescent Health, 18*, 211-217.

McConaughy, S.H., & Skiba, R. J. (1993). Comorbidity of externalizing and internalizing problems. *School Psychology Review, 22*(3), 421-437.

Pithers, W.D., Gray, A., Busconi, A., & Houchens, P. (1998). Five empirically-derived subtypes of children with sexual behaviour problems: Characteristics potentially related to juvenile delinquency and adult criminality. *The Irish Journal of Psychology,19*(1), 49-67.

Putnam, F.W. (2003). Ten-year research update review: Child sexual abuse. *Journal of the American Academy of Child and Adolescent Psychiatry, 42*(3), 269-278.

Quay, H.C. (1972). Patterns of aggression, withdrawal, and immaturity. In H.C. Quay & J. S. Werry (Eds.), *Psychological disorders of childhood*. New York: John Wiley & Sons.

Thompson, R.J., Moran, T., & Sack, W.H. (1988). Sexual abuse in young children: Its clinical presentation and characteristic patterns. *Child Abuse & Neglect, 12*, 163-170.

doi:10.1300/J394v04n01_03

APPENDIX

Data Collection Sheet

FILE NO. _____

AGE: _____ GENDER: _____

RACE:
- ☐ EUROPEAN AMERICAN (CAUCASIAN)
- ☐ AFRICAN AMERICAN
- ☐ HISPANIC
- ☐ ASIAN OR PACIFIC ISLANDER
- ☐ AMERICAN INDIAN
- ☐ OTHER: _____

VICTIM TYPE:
- ☐ PRIMARY
- ☐ SECONDARY (RELATION TO PRIMARY VICTIM _____)

AGE AT TIME OF VICTIMIZATION:
- ☐ CHILD (AGE 0-12)
- ☐ ADOLESCENT (AGE 13-17)

EMOTIONAL/BEHAVIORAL FUNCTIONING: within last three months

- ☐ Temper tantrums
- ☐ Fighting
- ☐ Setting fires
- ☐ Doesn't follow 1st req.
- ☐ Running away
- ☐ Depression/Sadness
- ☐ Excessive talking
- ☐ Loses things
- ☐ Extreme shyness
- ☐ Clingy/whiny
- ☐ Thumbsucking
- ☐ Physical complaints
- ☐ Increased eating
- ☐ Decreased eating
- ☐ Suicidal talk
- ☐ Suicidal attempts

- ☐ Destructiveness
- ☐ Lying
- ☐ Talking back
- ☐ Skips school
- ☐ Easily distracted
- ☐ Fidgety
- ☐ Spaces out/daydreams
- ☐ Excessive crying
- ☐ Fears or worries
- ☐ Baby talk
- ☐ Refusing to bathe
- ☐ Bladder cont. problems
- ☐ Bowel cont. problems
- ☐ Alcohol/Drugs
- ☐ Sexual acting out

- ☐ Hurtful to animals
- ☐ Hurtful to people
- ☐ Argumentative
- ☐ Stealing
- ☐ Lack of friends
- ☐ Interrupts others
- ☐ Hyperactive
- ☐ Imaginary friends
- ☐ Won't sleep alone
- ☐ Nightmares
- ☐ Sleep problems
- ☐ Excessive washing
- ☐ Accident prone
- ☐ Self-harmful
- ☐ Excessive masturbation

PROBLEMATIC SEXUAL BEHAVIORS? ☐ yes ☐ no

Stress and Strain
Among Personal Care Assistants
at an Assisted Living Facility

Kelsie R. Scott, BSSW
Kimberly McClure Cassie, MSSW, MA

SUMMARY. Personal care assistants at assisted living facilities are responsible for providing residents with a variety of services including personal care, housekeeping, laundry, meal service, and activity programming. Staff often perform these responsibilities with limited training and education while under the burden of heavy workloads. This paper explores the stress and strain experienced by personal care assistants at one assisted living facility. Particular attention is given to the difference between the stress and strain experienced by personal care assistants caring for people with dementia compared to those that work with people who do not suffer from a memory related disorder. Findings reveal staff caring for people with dementia experience more stress in the area of work constraints and interpersonal conflict at work. Differences between the stress and strain of personal care assistants surveyed and the norms found among employees at other workplaces are also discussed. doi:10.1300/J394v04n01_04 *[Article copies available for a fee from The Haworth Document Delivery Service: 1-800-HAWORTH. E-mail address:*

Kelsie R. Scott and Kimberly McClure Cassie are affiliated with The University of Tennessee, College of Social Work, 303 Henson Hall, Knoxville, TN 37996 (E-mail: kmcclur@utk.edu).

[Haworth co-indexing entry note]: "Stress and Strain Among Personal Care Assistants at an Assisted Living Facility" Scott, Kelsie R., and Kimberly McClure Cassie. Co-published simultaneously in *Journal of Evidence-Based Social Work* (The Haworth Press, Inc.) Vol. 4, No. 1/2, 2007, pp. 47-59; and: *Building Excellence: The Rewards and Challenges of Integrating Research into the Undergraduate Curriculum* (ed: Catherine N. Dulmus, and Karen M. Sowers) The Haworth Press, 2007, pp. 47-59. Single or multiple copies of this article are available for a fee from The Haworth Document Delivery Service [1-800-HAWORTH, 9:00 a.m. - 5:00 p.m. (EST). E-mail address: docdelivery@haworthpress.com].

KEYWORDS. Personal care assistants, interpersonal conflict, elderly, stress, dementia

INTRODUCTION

In recent years, staffing issues in nursing homes have received a great deal of attention from researchers, policy makers, and advocacy groups around the world in an effort to improve resident outcomes (Castle & Engberg, 2006; Dorr, Horn, & Smout, 2005; Horn, Smout, Buerhaus, Bergstrom, 2005; Matthew, 2005; Mueller, Arling, Kane, Bershadsky, Holland, & Joy, 2006). Staffing in assisted living facilities has not received the same attention. Despite the wide spread growth of assisted living communities in the United States over the past two decades, little attention has been focused on staff in assisted living facilities and their influence on resident outcomes. Since the mid-1980s there has been a tremendous growth in assisted living facilities in the United States with an estimated growth rate of 15 to 20% every year (National Center for Assisted Living, 1998; Spillman, Liu, & McGilliard, 1998). Because of the variation in the definition of assisted living from state to state, it is difficult to know precisely how many assisted living facilities exist in the United Stated today. Some estimates include small boarding homes serving fewer than six residents in their count of assisted living facilities (Assisted Living Federation of America, 1998; Mollica, 2000). These estimates report that there are 32,000 to 40,000 assisted living facilities in the country; however, when only those facilities housing ten or more residents are considered (Hawes, Rose, & Phillips, 1999), there appears to be about 11,500 assisted living facilities in the United States with the capacity to serve approximately 611,000 residents.

In contrast to traditional nursing homes, assisted living facilities tend to cater to older adults with fewer cognitive and physical deficits. In addition to basic housing, assisted living facilities typically provide nutritious meals, housekeeping and laundry services, as well as minimal assistance with activities of daily living, including medication management, bathing, dressing, and grooming. According to the National Center for Assisted Living (2001), 86% of residents in assisted living facilities require assistance with medication management, 72% with bathing, 57% with dressing, 41% with toileting, 35% with transfers and 23% with eating. Direct care providers, commonly referred to as personal care assistants at assisted living facilities, usually provide the majority of care to residents. In a national survey of 569 staff employed at assisted living facilities, researchers found that almost 97% of those that provided or supervised personal care activities were female and 68% were Caucasian (Hawes, Phillips & Rose, 2000). Hawes and colleagues also found that despite the fact that most staff were trained or licensed to provide personal care services to residents, many staff possessed only a limited understanding of the characteristics associated with normal aging. For example, more than three quarters of the staff sampled thought memory loss, incontinence, and depression were normal losses experienced by the elderly. Failure to accurately understand typical and atypical characteristics associated with normal age associated changes could jeopardize the health and mental health of many residents and could potentially increase the stress and strain experienced by personal care assistants.

Hawes and colleagues (2000) found that most staff in assisted living facilities were expected to perform a variety of activities. More specifically, the researchers noted that more than 90% of staff in assisted living facilities were expected to provide personal care to residents in need of assistance. More than 75% were expected to assist with activity programming and provide supervision or assistance with medication administration. In addition, almost 70% served meals, 60% provided laundry services, and over 50% performed housekeeping duties. The median workload was one personal care aide to 14 residents with some ratios as high as 1:23 or greater, however most staff did not perceive their workload to be heavy. Given the various responsibilities expected of personal care assistants in assisted living facilities we wonder how much stress and strain is experienced by these direct care providers and how that stress and strain affects resident outcomes. Because of the limited research on the subject in assisted living facilities, consideration of staffing issues in a similar industry, such as nursing homes, may provide additional insight into the stress and strain experienced by staff in assisted living facilities.

It has been estimated that direct care staff in nursing homes provide 80 to 90% of daily care to residents, but with turnover rates reaching 400% in some facilities, it is obvious that many direct care providers are unhappy with their jobs (Riggs & Rantz, 2001). Redfern, Hannon, Norman, and Martin (2002) found that a significant number of staff were dissatisfied with their jobs, but those who reported lower levels of stress in their jobs were more satisfied and more committed to their jobs. In Northern Italy, for example, researchers found that staff caring for older adults, especially staff with no professional training, experienced high levels of stress and burnout (Cocco, Gatti, Lima, & Camus, 2003). Similarly, Morgan, Semchuk, Stewart, and D'Arcy (2002) found that nursing assistants in rural Canadian nursing homes were more likely to experience higher levels of strain than other employees in the facility. As a result, resident care and the quality of life for residents are likely to suffer. Chou, Boldy, and Lee (2003) found staff satisfaction at Australian residential care facilities to be directly related to resident satisfaction. Because of the interrelationship between resident and staff satisfaction, it is imperative for social workers and other health care professionals to better understand the stress and strain experienced by direct care staff and its effect on resident outcomes in long-term residential care facilities.

Stress and strain among direct care providers in long-term residential care facilities comes from a variety of sources. Cohen-Mansfield (1989) found heavy workloads and interpersonal problems between co-workers and supervisors accounted for the negative attitudes of nursing home staff in her study of stress in an American nursing home. Similarly, staff surveyed at a British nursing home by Redfern and colleagues (2002) reported that the greatest stress on their job came from problems with interpersonal relationships at work, such as backbiting and disagreements among employees. Others have found heavy workloads, insufficient training and inadequate staffing among the sources of strain reported by nursing assistants (Morgan et al., 2002). As a result of increased strain, nursing assistants are more likely to have rushed encounters with residents. Morgan and colleagues found that nursing assistants under strain were more likely to do things for residents, rather than provide residents with verbal cues and assistance that could empower residents to perform their own activities of daily living. The consequence was increased frustration and decreased dignity among residents, as well as decreased job satisfaction among staff.

Those caring for people with dementia appear to be especially susceptible to high levels of job related stress. Researchers found that direct care staff have difficulty dealing with a variety of behavior problems manifested in people with dementia including aggression, resistance to care, memory problems, and wandering (Brodaty, Draper & Low, 2003; Schonfeld, 2003). Gates, Fitzwater, and Succop (2003) found that direct care staff experienced 624 assaults from residents over a ten-day period of time in their study of 138 nursing assistants at six nursing homes in Ohio. Assaults included, but were not limited to, being hit, pinched, kicked, scratched, and bitten by residents. People with dementia perpetrated 87% of the assaults on the direct care staff. Employees that experienced assaults reported increased job strain and heavy workloads with a smaller number of staff assigned to care for a larger number of residents.

Gruss, McCann, Edelman, and Farran (2004) examined job stress among direct care staff on two dementia care units in a long-term care facility. Staff on one unit were empowered to decide resident schedules, develop relationships with residents' families and to participate in resident activity programs, while staff on the other unit engaged in more traditional, task-focused responsibilities with little autonomy. Researchers found that both groups experienced stress at work, but those on the empowered unit experienced more resident centered stress revolving around issues such as accidents, behavior problems, and death and dying situations among residents. Those on the more traditional unit experienced more job focused stressors revolving around issues such as low salary compensation, heavy workloads, and interpersonal conflicts with coworkers.

This body of knowledge leads us to wonder whether or not personal care assistants in assisted living facilities, particularly those caring for people with dementia, experience stress and strain like their counterparts in nursing homes. More specifically, we want to know whether or not there is a difference between the stress and strain experienced by these personal care assistants caring for people with dementia and personal care assistants who do not care for people with dementia. This research will examine these questions.

Four hypotheses drive this study. First, we hypothesized that personal care assistants caring for people with dementia would encounter more constraints as they perform their job responsibilities than those that do not care for people with dementia. Secondly, we expected personal care assistants caring for people with dementia would experience more interpersonal conflict at work than those that do not care for people with dementia. Third, we expected personal care assistants caring for people with dementia would experience greater workloads than those that do not care for people with dementia. Finally, we hypothesize that personal care assistants caring for people with dementia will experience greater job strain as evidenced by greater physical symptoms than those that do not care for people with dementia.

METHODOLOGY

Data Collection

This study was conducted at one assisted living community located in a suburban area of the southeastern United States where the primary author completed a senior field placement. The assisted living community surveyed in this study had a general housing area where older adults that are able to live independently with limited assistance reside. The community also had several special care units dedicated to the care of assisted living residents with Alzheimer's disease or related disorders. Personal care assistants from both the general housing area and the special dementia care units were verbally invited to participate in the study. Those who chose to participate were provided with a survey that they could complete and anonymously return.

Measurements

Several measurements were obtained to test our hypotheses. Standard demographic information, including gender, ethnicity, and age, was obtained and participants were asked to indicate whether or not they worked in a dementia care unit or the general residence of the assisted living facility. In addition, three scales were used to examine the difference between stress experienced by personal care assistants caring for people with dementia and those that did not (Organizational Constraints Scale, Interpersonal Conflict at Work Scale, and the Quantitative Workload Inventory) and one scale was used to examine strain among respondents (Physical Symptoms Inventory). In their 1998 meta-analysis, Spector and Jex indicated each of these scales were developed by them for use in previous research (see Spector, 1987 and Spector, Dwyer, & Jex, 1988); however, their 1998 meta-analysis provides the most valuable information about the use and validity of these scales which will be discussed later in this section.

Organizational Constraints Scale. To begin, the Organizational Constraints Scale (OCS) was used to measure constraints that were reported to interfere with the work performance of personal care assistants. The OCS asked respondents to rate the frequency in which they encounter difficulty performing their job responsibilities based on constraints identified by Peters and O'Connor (1980). Potential constraints included the availability and quality of equipment and supplies, organizational policies and procedures, training and education, conflicting job demands, work interruptions and assistance from colleagues. Respondents could select one of five options to indicate the frequency with which they encountered each of the 11 constraints: less than once a month; once or twice a month; once or twice a week; once or twice a day; or several times every day. Each participant's response was summed with scores ranging from 11 to 55. Higher scores indicated more constraints on the employee's ability to perform his or her job responsibilities. Previous research by Spector and Jex (1998) indicates the norm for this scale was 21.3.

The Interpersonal Conflict at Work Scale. The Interpersonal Conflict at Work Scale (ICAWS) was used to measure the frequency with which personal care assistants encountered conflict with others at their place of employment. The ICAWS asked respondents to report how often they: (1) were involved in arguments with others at work; (2) were yelled at by people at work; (3) encountered rudeness at work; and (4) had nasty things done to them at work. Respondents could select one of five frequencies for these items: never, rarely, sometimes, quite often, or very often. Responses were summed and could range from 4-20, with larger scores indicating more conflict with others at work. The norm for this scale was 7.1 (Spector & Jex, 1998).

Quantitative Workload Inventory. The final stress measure used in this study was the Quantitative Workload Inventory (QWI), a five-item scale measuring the perceived volume of work, work pace, and job demands required of employees. Again, respondents were asked to report the frequency with which they experienced various workload demands based on options ranging from less than once a month to several times each day. Responses were summed with scores ranging from 5 to 25. Higher scores indicated greater workload. The norm for this scale was 16.5 (Spector & Jex, 1998).

Spector and Jex (1998) conducted a meta-analysis of 18 studies to examine the validity of these scales. Careers included in the studies varied from teachers to secretaries, nurses, social workers, policemen, firemen and others. Most of these studies examined workplaces in the eastern United States. Spector and Jex found good internal consistency and a moderate level of convergent validity among the three scales indicating objectivity was present among these self-report measures. All three measures were related to role conflict, while the ICAWS also correlated with organizational constraints, intention to leave, anxiety and depression. The QWI was also related to employee frustration.

Physical Symptoms Inventory. The Physical Symptoms Inventory (PSI) measured the number of health complaints experience by personal care assistants over the past 30 days. The PSI provided respondents with a list of 18 conditions ranging from gastrointestinal complaints and cardiovascular complaints to headaches and skin rashes. Respondents were asked to indicate whether or not they experienced each of the conditions listed and whether or not they saw a physician for the conditions they experienced. The PSI was designed to provide researchers with three scores. The first score provided researchers with the total number of physical symptoms experienced by a participant for which they did not seek medical treatment. The second score indicated the total number of physical symptoms for which a respondent sought treatment from a physician. The final score was a sum of the first two scores or a total number of symptoms experienced that did or did not require treatment from a physician. For the purpose of this study, only the final score was considered. The final score could range from 0-18. The norm for the total score on the PSI was 5.4 (Spector & Jex, 1998). Data obtained from all completed surveys was analyzed using frequency distributions and Mann-Whitney comparisons.

RESULTS

Sample Characteristics

Twenty-one personal care assistants participated in the study. Ten of the participants cared for people with dementia and the remaining 11 cared for individuals that did not have dementia in the general housing population of the assisted living community. All of the participants were female and all but one identified themselves as Caucasian. The remaining participant was African American. The average age of the participants was 35.

Organizational Constraints

Our first hypothesis was supported. Results indicated a statistically significant difference existed between the organizational constraints experienced by those that did and did not care for people with dementia (Mann-Whitney $U = 19.0$, $Z = -2.59$, $p = .01$). The average OCS score for those caring for people with dementia was 14.6 compared to only 7.73 for those caring for general assisted living residents. Results for this and other measurements are summarized in Table 1.

TABLE 1. Summary of Stress and Strain Scores

Measurement	Norm Score	Mean Score for Dementia Caregivers	Mean Score for Non Dementia Caregivers	Mann Whitney
Organizational Constraints Scale	21.3	14.6	7.73	19*
Interpersonal Conflict at Work Scale	7.1	15.45	6.95	10.5**
Quantitative Workload Inventory	16.5	11.55	10.5	49.5
Physical Symptoms Inventory	5.4	10.95	11.05	54.5

$*p = .01 **p < .001$

Interpersonal Conflict

Results also supported our second hypothesis. Personal care assistants caring for people with dementia experienced more interpersonal conflict at work than those that did not care for people with dementia (Mann-Whitney $U = 10.5$, $Z = -3.31$, $p = .001$). More specifically, the average ICAWS score for those caring for people with dementia was 15.45 compared to only 6.95 for those that did not care for people with dementia.

Workload

The third hypothesis was not supported in our data analysis. There was not a statistically significant difference between the workload of the two groups. The average QWI of those working with people with dementia was 10.5 compared to 11.55 among those working with the general assisted living population.

Strain

The final hypothesis was also not supported. There was no statistically significant difference between the strain expressed by personal care assistants caring for people with dementia and those working with the general assisted living population. The average number of physical symptoms experienced by those caring for people with dementia was 10.95. The average number of physical symptoms experienced by personal care assistants working in the general assisted living population was slightly higher at 11.5.

DISCUSSION

Findings indicated personal care assistants caring for people with dementia experienced greater levels of stress in the areas of organizational constraints and interpersonal conflict than personal care assistants working in the general assisted living population with residents that did not suffer from dementia related disorders at the surveyed community. Given the behavior problems, mood changes and resistance to care that is common among people with dementia, it is reasonable to expect personal care assistants working with people with dementia to experience more constraints and conflict as their perform their job responsibilities. Such stress among personal care assistants working with people with dementia could possibly result in negative care outcomes, decreased quality of life, and in some extreme cases, resident abuse. Higher turnover rates and associated financial costs to the organization to recruit and train new employees is also likely to occur as a result of increased stress among personal care assistants caring for people with dementia. Assisted living facilities should be encouraged to look for ways to decrease stress among employees and offer stress reduction workshops and services to employees.

Interestingly, the ICAWS scores for personal care assistants caring for people with dementia and the OCS scores of both groups were well below norms reported by Spector and Jex (1998). This could lead one to question whether or not the organizational policies and procedures, employee training programs, and supervision provided by the administration of this assisted living community might be more supportive than the organization culture of other work environments. Additional research would be needed to confirm this supposition.

Similarly, it is also interesting to note that the QWI scores of this sample were also well below the norm reported by Spector and Jex (1998), suggesting personal care assistants at this assisted living community experienced less workload burden than those in other work environments. It would be useful to know the past work history of the personal care assistants at this community. It would be reasonable to expect that those previously employed as skilled nursing assistants in nursing homes where residents tend to be more dependent upon staff, might see the shift to employment in an assisted living facility as a decrease in workload. For example, a significant number of residents in nursing homes are completely bedridden and dependent upon staff for turning and repositioning in the bed and complete body lifts when transferring a resident from the bed to a chair. In an assisted living facility, residents are generally required to be somewhat independent with mobility. A nursing assistant accustomed to caring for residents that are totally reliant upon staff for most care in a nursing home, may see a shift to an assisted living facility as a reduction in workload demands. Replication is necessary to confirm whether or not personal care assistants do indeed experience lighter workloads than the general workforce and if so, how and why this could occur.

Finally, while there was no difference in the job strain of personal care assistants caring for people with dementia and those working with the general population at this assisted living facility, it is interesting to note that the personal care assistants surveyed experienced what appears to be a significantly greater amount of physical symptoms ($M = 11$) than the norm ($M = 5$) reported by Spector and Jex (1998). Given the physical demands associated with providing elders with assistance in the areas of bathing, dressing, and grooming, and the emotional demands associated with demanding behavior, repetitive questions and safety issues encountered when working with people with dementia, it is easy to understand why job strain is so high among personal care assistants. It would be interesting to examine physical and emotional demands separately in future research to see if there is a difference between the amount of physical and emotional strain experienced by personal care assistants caring for people with dementia compared to those that do not work with people with dementia. It would be reasonable to expect personal care assistants caring for people with dementia to experience more emotional strain because of the many problematic behaviors and safety issues associated with caring for those with memory problems.

CONCLUSION

While the sample in this study was somewhat small and confined to only one facility, findings suggest that individuals caring for people with dementia experience more interpersonal conflict and organizational constraints than those who do not work with people with dementia. Additional research is needed before these findings can be generalized to the greater population. While strain and workload were not significant in this study, these variables should continue to be explored in future research to see if differences may exist when analyzing a larger sample. Additional variables that could contribute to these findings, such as length of time with the organization, staff to resident ratios, prior experience, and previous education or training, should also be examined.

Given that staff in this survey reported more health complaints than staff in other studies future research should consider whether or not these health complaints could be representative of regional health disparities or some other factor. Future research should also examine how job stress among personal care assistants is related to resident outcomes, such as declines in activities of daily living and quality of life. It would also be useful to examine the success or failure of organizational interventions designed to reduce job stress among staff at assisted living facilities. Additional research in needed in these areas to improve the quality of care and resident outcomes in assisted living facilities.

REFERENCES

Assisted Living Federation of America. (1998). *The assisted living industry: An overview–1998*. Fairfax, VA: Price Waterhouse for ALFA.

Brodaty, H., Draper, B., & Low, L.F. (2003). Nursing home staff attitudes towards residents with dementia: Strain and satisfaction with work. *Journal of Advanced Nursing*, *44*(6), 583-590.

Castle, N.G., & Engberg, J. (2006). Organizational characteristics associated with staff turnover in nursing homes. *The Gerontologist*, *46*, 62-73.

Chou, S.C., Boldy, D.P., & Lee, A.H. (2003). Factors influencing residents' satisfaction in residential aged care. *The Gerontologist*, *43*(4), 459-472.

Cocco, E., Gatti, M., Lima, C.A.M., & Camus, V. (2003). A comparative study of stress and burnout among staff caregivers in nursing homes and acute geriatric wards. *International Journal of Geriatric Psychiatry*, *18*, 78-85.

Cohen-Mansfield, J. (1989). Sources of satisfaction and stress in nursing home caregivers: Preliminary results. *Journal of Advanced Nursing*, *14*, 383-388.

Dorr, D.A., Horn, S.D., & Smout, R.J. (2005). Cost analysis of nursing home registered nurse staffing times. *Journal of the American Geriatrics Society*, *53*(3), 840-845.

Gates, D., Fitzwater, E., & Succop, P. (2003). Relationships of stressors, strain, and anger to caregiver assaults. *Issues in Mental Health Nursing*, *24*, 775-793.

Gruss, V., McCann, J. J., Edelman, P., & Farran, C. J. (2004). Job stress among nursing home certified nursing assistants. *Alzheimer's Care Quarterly*, *5*(3), 207-216.

Hawes, C., Rose, M., & Phillips, C. (1999). *A national study of assisted living for the frail elderly, executive summary: Results of a national survey of facilities*. Beachwood, OH: Myers Research Institute. Retrieved July 17, 2005 from http://aspe.hhs.gov/daltcp/reports/facres.htm

Hawes, C., Phillips, C.D., & Rose, M. (2000). *High Service or high privacy assisted living facilities, their residents and staff: Results from a national survey*. Washington, DC: US Department of Health and Human Services. Retrieved July 17, 2005 from http://aspe.hhs.gov/daltcp/reportes/hshp.htm

Horn, S.D., Smout, R.J., Buerhaus, P., Bergstrom, N. (2005). RN staffing times and outcomes of long-stay nursing home residents. *The American Journal of Nursing*, *105*(11), 58-70.

Matthew, M. (2005). Nursing home staffing. *The American Journal of Nursing, 105*(12), 15-16.

Mollica, R. (2000). *State Assisted Living Policy.* Portland, ME: National Academy for State Health Policy. Retrieved July 27, 2005 from http://aspe.hhs.gov/daltcp/reports/98state.htm

Morgan, D.G., Semchuk, K.M., Stewart, N.J., & D'Arcy, C. (2002). Job strain among staff of rural nursing homes. *Journal of Nursing Administration, 32*(3), 152-161.

Mueller, C., Arling, G., Kane, R., Bershadsky, J., Holland, D., & Joy, A. (2006). Nursing home staffing standards: Their relationship to nurse staffing levels. *The Gerontologist, 46,* 74-80.

National Center for Assisted Living. (1998). 1998 Facts and Trends: *The assisted living sourcebook.* Washington, DC: National Center for Assisted Living & American Health Care Association.

National Center for Assisted Living. (2001). 2001 Facts and Trends: *The assisted living sourcebook.* Washington, DC: National Center for Assisted Living.

Peters, L.H., & O'Connor, E. J. (1980). Situational constraints and work outcomes: The influences of a frequently overlooked construct. *Academy of Management Review, 5,* 391-397.

Redfern, S., Hannan, S., Norman, I., & Martin, F. (2002). Work satisfaction, stress, quality of care and morale of older people in a nursing home. *Health and Social Care in the Community, 10*(6), 512-517.

Riggs, C.J., & Rantz, M.J. (2001). A model of staff support to improve retention in long-term care. *Nursing Administration, 25*(92), 43-53.

Schonfeld, L. (2003). Behavior problems in assisted living facilities. *The Journal of Applied Gerontology, 22*(4), 490-505.

Spector, P.E. (1987). Interactive effects of perceived control and job stressors on affective reactions and health outcomes for clerical workers. *Work and Stress, 1,* 155-162.

Spector, P.E., Dwyer, D.J., & Jex, S.M. (1988). Relation of job stressors to affective, health, and performance outcomes: A comparison of multiple data sources. *Journal of Applied Psychology, 73,* 11-19.

Spector, P.E., & Jex, S.M. (1998). Development of four self-reported measures of job stressors and strain: Interpersonal Conflict at Work Scale, Organizational Constraints Scale, Quantitative Workload Inventory, and Physical Symptoms Inventory. *Journal of Occupational Health Psychology, 3*(4), 356-367.

Spillman, B.C., Liu, K., & McGilliard, C. (2002). *Trends in Residential Long-Term Care: Use of Nursing Homes and Assisted Living and Characteristics of Facilities and Residents.* Washington, DC: US Department of Health and Human Services. Retrieved July 17, 2005 from http://aspe.hhs.gov/daltcp/reports/rltct.htm

doi:10.1300/J394v04n01_04

The Relationship Between Childhood Abuse and Adult Suicidal Behavior Among Rural Former Mental Health Patients

Karen E. Richards, BSSW
Irma A. Molina, MSW

SUMMARY. This article explores the relationship between childhood abuse and adult suicidal behavior among former mental health patients in a rural area. Historical data from 1999-2005 were used and analyzed from an outpatient mental health center. Suicidal ideation and attempts were found to be significantly correlated to all types of childhood abuse, such as mental, physical, and sexual. We conclude with recommendations for future research and implications for future social work practice. doi:10.1300/J394v04n01_05 *[Article copies available for a fee from The Haworth Document Delivery Service: 1-800-HAWORTH. E-mail address: <docdelivery@haworthpress.com> Website: <http://www.HaworthPress.com> © 2007 by The Haworth Press, Inc. All rights reserved.]*

KEYWORDS. Childhood abuse, suicidal ideation, mental health, rural

Karen E. Richards is affiliated with The University of Tennessee, College of Social Work, Knoxville, TN 37996 (E-mail: krichar2@utk.edu).

Irma A. Molina is a Doctoral Student, The University of Tennessee, College of Social Work, 4 Henson Hall, Knoxville, TN 37996 (E-mail: imolina@utk.edu).

[Haworth co-indexing entry note]: "The Relationship Between Childhood Abuse and Adult Suicidal Behavior Among Rural Former Mental Health Patients." Richards, Karen E., and Irma A. Molina. Co-published simultaneously in *Journal of Evidence-Based Social Work* (The Haworth Press, Inc.) Vol. 4, No. 1/2, 2007, pp. 61-78; and: *Building Excellence: The Rewards and Challenges of Integrating Research into the Undergraduate Curriculum* (ed: Catherine N. Dulmus, and Karen M. Sowers) The Haworth Press, 2007, pp. 61-78. Single or multiple copies of this article are available for a fee from The Haworth Document Delivery Service [1-800-HAWORTH, 9:00 a.m. - 5:00 p.m. (EST). E-mail address: docdelivery@haworthpress.com].

INTRODUCTION

In the United States in the year 2002, suicide was the leading cause of death among persons aged 25-34 and the third leading cause of death for those aged 10-24. It remained in the top five leading cause of death for persons aged 10-54 years of age for the year 2002. In 2001, suicide took the lives of 30,622 people; in 2002, 132,353 individuals were hospitalized following suicide attempts; 116,639 were treated in emergency departments and released (Centers for Disease Control and Prevention [CDC], 2004). In 2001 there were 30,000 suicides in the United States or 83 suicides a day which means every 17 minutes an individual takes his or her life (National Center for Health Statistics, 2004). Statistics also show that suicide among the elderly particularly among those 65 years and older are very high, although suicide was not the leading cause of death for this age group. Most elderly suicide victims are seen by their primary care provider a few weeks before their suicide attempt and diagnosed with mild to moderate depression. Although males are four times more likely to die of suicide than females, females are more likely to attempt suicide than males. Among young people, the suicide rate has increased dramatically. From 1952-1996, the incidence of suicide among adolescents and young adults have nearly tripled. From 1980-1996, suicide rates increased 14% and 100% among persons aged 15-19 years and 10-14 years, respectively (DHHS, 2005). In the 1997 Youth Risk Behavior Survey of US high school students, 12% of girls and 4.5% of boys reported suicide attempts (CDC, 1998). With these alarming statistics, it is imperative to determine indicators and risk factors for suicide, so appropriate interventions can be established.

CHILDHOOD ABUSE AND PSYCHOPATHOLOGY IN ADULTHOOD

It has been demonstrated in various empirical studies that there are more reports of self-harm, suicidal ideation, and suicidal behavior in clinical and community populations of adults who report sexual and/or physical abuse in childhood than in comparison groups who do not report abuse (Santa Mina & Gallop, 1998). Numerous studies among college students (Peters & Range, 1995; Thakkar, Gutierrez, Kuczen, & McCanne, 2000; Stepakoff, 1998; Gibb, Alloy, Abramson, Rose, Whitehouse, & Hogan, 2001; Bryant & Range, 1995; Nilsen & Conner, 2002), in a community population of adults (Briere & Runtz, 1986;

Davidson, Hughes, George, & Blazer, 1996; Anderson, Tiro, Price, Bender, & Kaslow, 2002), and one study among pregnant women (Farber, Herbert, & Reviere, 1996) have demonstrated that a history of physical and/or sexual abuse predicted suicidal ideation or behavior. Childhood abuse has been linked with psychosocial problems in the abused individual both during childhood and adulthood (Lundqvist, Svedin, & Hansson, 2004; Osvath, Voros, & Fekete, 2004).

Various studies have demonstrated relationships between childhood abuse and adult disorders and psychopathology such as depression (Ernst, Angst, & Foldenyi, 1993; McCauley et al., 1997; Lundqvist et al., 2004; Ullman & Brecklin; McHolm, MacMillan, & Jamieson, 2003); low self-esteem and somatization (McCauley et al., 1997); substance abuse (McCauley et al.; Roy, 2001a; Roy, 2004; Rossow & Lauritzen, 2001; Ullman & Brecklin, 2002); bipolar disorder (Garno, Goldberg, Ramirez, & Ritzler, 2005; Soloff, Lynch, & Kelly, 2002); social phobia (Ernst et al., 1993); sexual problems (Ernst et al.; Lundqvist et al.); eating disorders (Lundqvist et al.); personality disorder (Lundqvist et al.); and posttraumatic stress disorder (Oquendo et al., 2005; Ullman & Brecklin; Davidson, Hughes, George, & Blazer, 1996).

Although the causal risk factors for suicide include psychiatric diagnoses of major depression, bipolar disorder, schizophrenia, alcohol and drug use disorders, and personality disorders, only a small portion of individuals with psychopathology take their own lives. Some of the constructs that have been consistently associated with completed suicide include impulsivity/aggression, depression, anxiety, hopelessness, and self-consciousness/social disengagement (Conner, Duberstein, Conwell, Seidlitz, & Caine, 2001). Some investigators have shown that mediating variables such as shame or self-blame (Barker-Collo, 2001; Whiffen & MacIntosh, 2005), interpersonal difficulties, and avoidant coping strategies (Whiffen & MacIntosh), and cognitive functioning (Yang & Clum, 2000) can affect the impact of emotional distress and trauma brought about by the abuse. Childhood trauma has been found to be a determinant of the age of onset of suicidal behavior and of the number of suicide attempts (Roy, 2004). In one study, hopelessness was 1.3 times more important than depression was for explaining suicidal ideation (Beck, Steer, Beck, & Newman, 1993). One study measured adulthood psychological outcomes by documenting the presence or absence of particular diagnoses and assessing the severity of psychological symptoms in female adult survivors of childhood sexual abuse. Characteristics associated with the sexual abuse by the first perpetrator predicted the development of bipolar disorder, major depressive episode, and agoraphobia, whereas any or total abuse variables were related to the development of BPD, substance abuse, MDE, suicidality, bulimia, and panic disorder. Violence against the father by the mother was associated with BPD, bulimia, agoraphobia, and PTSD. Substance abuse within the household was related to substance abuse, MDE, suicidality, bulimia, panic disorder, and PTSD. Maternal care and overprotection were related to substance abuse and PTSD (Katerndahl, Burge, & Kellogg, 2005). It has also been reported that factors such as multiple maltreatment (Bryant & Range, 1995; Anderson et al., 2002), sexual maltreatment/intercourse (Bryant & Range; Briere & Runtz, 1986) and multiple perpetrators and concurrent physical abuse (Briere & Runtz, 1986) are more damaging in terms of suicidality.

CHILDHOOD ABUSE AND SUICIDE

As far back as the 1970s the general public, healthcare workers, legislative, judicial, law enforcement, and the media have been under the assumption that child abuse had a relationship to suicide (Rind, Tromovitch, & Bauserman, 1998).

Individuals with a childhood history of sexual or physical abuse have been found to be at greater risk for adult self-harm, suicidal ideations, and suicidal behaviors (McHolm, MacMillan, & Jamieson, 2003). Previous researches have shown that suicidality may be influenced by a variety of factors such as sex, age, marital status, race, and psychiatric disorders especially depression and post-traumatic stress disorders. Negative life events in childhood, such as child physical or sexual abuse can have a variety of negative outcomes, such as suicide among adolescents and adults as well as adult psychopathology. Browne and Finkelhor (1986) identified self-harm and suicide as symptoms of psychopathology following childhood abuse.

A review of 29 studies conducted from 1988-1998 illustrated a relationship between childhood physical and sexual abuse and adult self-harm, suicidal ideation, and suicide attempt, and completed suicide. The odds of suicide attempts among adults sexually abused in childhood were estimated to be 1.3 to 25.6 higher than for those not sexually abused. The authors concluded that the role of childhood trauma as causal or contributing factors to adult self-destructive acts is not well understood (Santa Mina & Gallop, 1998).

It has been reported that the risks for attempted suicide increased substantially from 2-5-fold for each adverse childhood experiences (e.g., abuse and neglect). As the number of such experiences increased, the risk of ever attempting suicide, as well as attempted suicide during either childhood/adolescence or adulthood, increased dramatically (Dube, Anda, Felitti, Chapman, Williamson, & Giles, 2001).

Table 1 shows that of the 83 clients who experienced sexual abuse, 72 had suicidal ideations. The chi-square test also shows that clients who have reported sexual abuse were more likely to report adult suicidal ideation ($p < .001$).

Data from the National Comorbidity Survey indicated a strong association between child sexual abuse and suicidal behavior, mediated by psychopathology. There was a strong relationship between child sexual abuse and most major psychiatric disorders such as such as mood, anxiety, and substance use disorders among men and women. The prevalence of suicidal behaviors among those who experienced child sexual abuse was significantly higher than the prevalence of those not reporting child sexual abuse. It was also reported that among those sexually abused as children, odds of suicide attempts were 2-4 times higher among women

TABLE 1. Relationship Between Suicidal Ideation and Sexual Abuse

Crosstab

Count

| | | Sex abuse | | Total |
		no	yes	
suicidal ideation	no	52	11	63
	yes	65	72	137
Total		117	83	200

Chi-Square Tests

	Value	df	Asymp. Sig. (2-sided)	Exact Sig. (2-sided)	Exact Sig. (1-sided)
Pearson Chi-Square	21.893(b)	1	.000		
Continuity Correction(a)	20.471	1	.000		
Likelihood Ratio	23.534	1	.000		
Fisher's Exact Test				.000	.000
N of Valid Cases	200				

a Computed only for a 2 x 2 table
b 0 cells (.0%) have expected count less than 5. The minimum expected count is 26.15.

and 4-11 times higher among men, compared with those not abused. Seventy-nine percent of serious suicide attempts among women could be attributed to psychiatric disorders while 12% was attributable to rape and 7% to molestation (Molnar, Buka, & Kessler, 2001).

Table 2 shows the relationship between suicidal ideation and physical abuse. Seventy-six clients have experienced physical abuse and the majority (66 clients) reported suicidal ideation. Of the 124 clients who reported no physical abuse in childhood, more than half (71 clients) also reported suicidal ideation. Clients who report childhood physical abuse were more likely to report adult suicidal ideation ($p < .001$).

A study conducted with subjects in a general hospital admitted due to suicide attempt indicated that a childhood history of sexual and physical abuse made independent contributions to repeated suicide attempts when controlling for a wide range of other childhood adversities such as parental loss, neglect, antipathy, and severe discord in the family (Ystgaard, Hestetun, Loeb, & Mehlum, 2004).

A 10-year longitudinal study of young Swiss adults illustrated that lifetime suicide attempts were five times more frequent among child

TABLE 2. Relationship Between Suicidal Ideation and Physical Abuse

Crosstab

Count

		Physical abuse		Total
		no	yes	
suicidal ideation	no	53	10	63
	yes	71	66	137
Total		124	76	200

Chi-Square Tests

	Value	df	Asymp. Sig. (2-sided)	Exact Sig. (2-sided)	Exact Sig. (1-sided)
Pearson Chi-Square	19.113(b)	1	.000		
Continuity Correction(a)	17.766	1	.000		
Likelihood Ratio	20.754	1	.000		
Fisher's Exact Test				.000	.000
N of Valid Cases	200				

a Computed only for a 2 x 2 table
b 0 cells (.0%) have expected count less than 5. The minimum expected count is 23.94.

sexual abuse cases than among controls. Child sexual abuse was also associated with major depression, and social phobia, and sexual problems (Ernst et al., 1993).

Table 3 shows that of the 24 clients who reported childhood mental abuse, all but one also reported suicidal ideation. The chi-square test result showed that the relationship between suicidal ideation and childhood mental abuse was significant ($p = .002$). Clients experiencing mental abuse were more likely to report adult suicidal ideation.

In Sweden, in a study conducted with adult female psychiatric outpatients who had been sexually abused in childhood reported that suicidal thoughts was the most frequent problem reported, which accounted for 87% of the women. Nearly half of the group had made one suicide attempt. At least one psychiatric diagnosis was recorded for all the women, with post-traumatic stress disorder recorded as the first diagnosis (Lundqvist et al., 2004).

A cohort of randomly selected children was studied during a 17-year period to determine the magnitude and independence of the effects of

TABLE 3. Relationship Between Suicidal Ideation and Mental Abuse

Crosstab

Count

		Mental abuse		Total
		no	yes	
suicidal ideation	no	62	1	63
	yes	114	23	137
Total		176	24	200

Chi-Square Tests

	Value	df	Asymp. Sig. (2-sided)	Exact Sig. (2-sided)	Exact Sig. (1-sided)
Pearson Chi-Square	9.443(b)	1	.002		
Continuity Correction(a)	8.058	1	.005		
Likelihood Ratio	12.511	1	.000		
Fisher's Exact Test				.002	.001
N of Valid Cases	200				

a Computed only for a 2 x 2 table
b 0 cells (.0%) have expected count less than 5. The minimum expected count is 7.56.

childhood neglect, physical abuse, and sexual abuse on adolescent and adult depression and suicidal behavior. It was found that adolescents and young adults with a history of child maltreatment were three times more likely to become depressed or suicidal compared with individuals without such a history. Risk of suicide attempts was also 8 times greater for youths with a sexual abuse history. Those individuals with sexual abuse history were at a greater risk of becoming depressed or suicidal during adolescence and young adulthood (Brown, Cohen, Johnson, & Smailes, 1999).

Table 4 shows that of the 83 clients who have reported childhood sexual abuse, more than half (52 clients) have attempted suicide. The chi-square test results show that those who have experienced childhood sexual abuse were more likely to report adult suicidal attempts ($p < .001$).

A study conducted among clients both men and women in a mental health center in New Zealand showed that current suicide risk was related to all four child abuse categories but was predicted better by child sexual abuse experienced on average 20 years previously, than by

TABLE 4. Relationship Between Suicide Attempt and Sexual Abuse

Crosstab

Count

		Sex abuse		Total
		no	yes	
suicide attempt	no	81	31	112
	yes	36	52	88
Total		117	83	200

Chi-Square Tests

	Value	df	Asymp. Sig. (2-sided)	Exact Sig. (2-sided)	Exact Sig. (1-sided)
Pearson Chi-Square	20.029(b)	1	.000		
Continuity Correction(a)	18.756	1	.000		
Likelihood Ratio	20.246	1	.000		
Fisher's Exact Test				.000	.000
N of Valid Cases	200				

a Computed only for a 2 x 2 table
b 0 cells (.0%) have expected count less than 5. The minimum expected count is 36.52.

a current diagnosis of depression (Read, Agar, Barker-Collo, Davies, & Moskowitz, 2001).

Historical as well as current research seems to overwhelmingly support child abuse as an indicator for suicide and suicidal ideations. Most studies reviewed, however, did not specifically focus on the geographical setting as urban or rural. Several studies conducted with community samples did not specify the type of geographical location of the community where the study was conducted (Briere & Runtz, 1986; Davidson et al., 1996; McHolm et al., 2003).

Table 5 shows that of the 76 clients who reported childhood physical abuse, more than half (43 clients) have attempted suicide in adulthood. The chi-test results show that clients with physical abuse experience in childhood were more likely to report suicide attempt in adulthood ($p = .005$).

The aim of this study is to examine the relationship between childhood abuse and adult suicidal behavior among former mental health patients in a rural setting. Little research has been focused on this group. Current research seems to be focusing on child abuse in relation to

TABLE 5. Relationship Between Suicide Attempt and Physical Abuse

Crosstab

Count

		Physical abuse		Total
		no	yes	
suicide attempt	no	79	33	112
	yes	45	43	88
Total		124	76	200

Chi-Square Tests

	Value	df	Asymp. Sig. (2-sided)	Exact Sig. (2-sided)	Exact Sig. (1-sided)
Pearson Chi-Square	7.872(b)	1	.005		
Continuity Correction(a)	7.070	1	.008		
Likelihood Ratio	7.876	1	.005		
Fisher's Exact Test				.006	.004
N of Valid Cases	200				

a Computed only for a 2 x 2 table
b 0 cells (.0%) have expected count less than 5. The minimum expected count is 33.44.

adult psychopathology or specific mental illness, or sub-groups, like women, men, or college students. Because of the lack of studies addressing the connection between child abuse and suicide specific to a particular geographic location, this is a research gap that needs to be filled.

In the context of this study, childhood abuse was defined as any actions–physical, mental, or sexual–that the patient perceives as abusive. Actions that were not perceived by the client as abusive even though they may have constituted childhood abuse as stipulated by law were not included as outcome measures in the study. Therefore, the patient's subjective perception of what constitutes childhood abuse was the sole criteria for defining childhood abuse. Suicidal behavior was defined as consisting of suicidal ideation, attempt, or completed suicide.

SUBJECTS AND METHODS

Subjects

This study used archival data drawn from closed case files at a rural mental health care facility. The data came from the records of former mental healthcare patients. A review of historical files was conducted and data were collected using patients' responses to initial intake assessments and disclosures during case management visits, therapy session, or medical examinations. The researcher used systematic sampling method by selecting every fifth record from the archived files. A total of 200 records were reviewed. The criteria for inclusion included: (1) patients 19 years of age and above; (2) residents of a certain geographic area; (3) a history of childhood abuse, physical, sexual, or mental; and (4) history of suicidal behavior or ideations in adulthood. Data collection covered a five-year period, from 1999-2005.

Statistical Methods

Suicidal behavior in adulthood was the dependent variable of interest in this study. They were categorized as suicidal ideation and suicide attempts. Suicidal ideation was defined as any thought or fantasy about committing suicide while suicide attempt was defined as any self-destructive act to end one's life. Reported childhood abuse was the primary independent variable. They were categorized as mental abuse, physical abuse, and sexual abuse. Childhood abuse, as defined in this study, refers to any actions–physical, mental, or sexual, that the patient perceives as abusive. Actions that were not perceived by the client as abusive even thought they may be stipulated by law as abusive acts were not included in the definition of childhood abuse.

Cross tabulations of the different abuses by suicide attempt and suicidal ideation were done by using SPSS 13. The results of the cross tabs tell how many people were victimized by each type of abuse and have attempted suicide or thought about it. Six different chi-square tests were also conducted (suicide ideation by physical, sexual, and mental abuse, and suicide attempts by physical, sexual, and mental abuse) to know the association among the different types of abuse to suicidal ideation or attempt.

Data Presentation and Analysis

Results

Crosstabs

Case Processing Summary

	Cases					
	Valid		Missing		Total	
	N	Percent	N	Percent	N	Percent
sui_idea * sex abuse	200	100.0%	0	.0%	200	100.0%
sui_idea * phy abuse	200	100.0%	0	.0%	200	100.0%
sui_idea * mental abuse	200	100.0%	0	.0%	200	100.0%
sui_attempt * sex abuse	200	100.0%	0	.0%	200	100.0%
sui_attempt * phy abuse	200	100.0%	0	.0%	200	100.0%
sui_attempt * mental abuse	200	100.0%	0	.0%	200	100.0%

Table 6 shows that of the 24 clients who experienced mental abuse in childhood, the majority (18 clients) have attempted suicide in adulthood. The relationship between suicide attempt and mental abuse was found to be significant from the chi-square test result ($p = .001$).

The results of the chi-square tests clearly show that any type of childhood abuse is significantly associated with adult suicidal behavior, either suicidal ideation or attempt. The majority of the clients who reported any form of childhood abuse (mental, physical, or sexual) also reported suicidal behavior in adulthood. All abuse variables were found to be significantly related too suicidal ideation and attempts.

TABLE 6. Relationship Between Suicide Attempt and Mental Abuse

Crosstab

Count

		Mentall abuse		Total
		no	yes	
suicide attempt	no	106	6	112
	yes	70	18	88
Total		176	24	200

Chi-Square Tests

	Value	df	Asymp. Sig. (2-sided)	Exact Sig. (2-sided)	Exact Sig. (1-sided)
Pearson Chi-Square	10.637(b)	1	.001		
Continuity Correction(a)	9.255	1	.002		
Likelihood Ratio	10.808	1	.001		
Fisher's Exact Test				.002	.001
N of Valid Cases	200				

a Computed only for a 2 x 2 table
b 0 cells (.0%) have expected count less than 5. The minimum expected count is 10.56.

More suicidal ideations have been reported than attempted suicide. This goes to show that not everyone who thought about committing suicide would actually attempt to do so. It is significant to note, however, that almost half of clients who reported any form of childhood abuse have attempted suicide.

The prevention of mental health problems in rural areas is therefore one area that should be looked into. Access to psychological services is of primary importance to insure the health and well-being of rural Americans since the leading causes of mortality and disability in rural America are, in large part, behavioral or lifestyles promoting chronic disease (American Psychological Association, 1995). There is stigma attached to having a mental disorder in rural areas and this can lead to under-diagnosis and under-treatment of mental disorders among rural residents (National Rural Health Association, 1999). It has also been reported that limited availability, accessibility, and acceptability of rural mental health services can have serious consequences for individuals and families in rural areas (Sawyer & Beeson, 1998).

DISCUSSION

Of the 200 records of clients analyzed in this study, 24 clients have reported childhood mental abuse, 76 had childhood physical abuse, and 83 had childhood sexual abuse. Adult suicidal ideation was reported by 137 clients and adult suicide attempts by 88 clients. The result of the study showed that a history of childhood abuse was significantly associated with suicidal ideation or attempt in adulthood. The chi-square test results showed that clients with a history of childhood abuse (mental, physical, or sexual) were more likely to report suicidal ideation and/or attempt in adulthood. The occurrence of any type of childhood abuse was associated with adult suicidal behavior, either suicidal ideation or actual attempt. The majority of the sample has experienced suicidal ideation and almost half have attempted suicide. It supports the finding that childhood abuse is related to suicidality in adulthood and that trauma in childhood can have a significant impact on adult behavior.

Considering the findings of this study, it is important for mental health clinics to consider a client's history of childhood abuse when assessing suicide risk. Mental health clinics should also offer services to help clients deal with both their past abuse and current suicidal behaviors. It will also enhance the assessment of adult suicidality, based on the knowledge on a client's abuse history.

Methodological Limitations

Although this study was able to link childhood abuse and adult suicidal behavior, it was not possible to verify the reported abuse of the clients. The data used were taken from client files and since abuse and suicidal behaviors were based from client self-reports, the reliability of the data is in question. Clients may have overreported or underreported their abuse histories. Their disclosures of abuse were not also validated from other sources. No standard definition of what constitutes the different types of abuse was used as abuse was defined based on the client's subjective perception of what constitutes an abuse. Childhood abuse was defined as any actions–physical, mental, or sexual–that he/she perceives as abusive. Actions that were not perceived by the client as abusive even though they may have constituted childhood abuse as stipulated by law were not included. In the same vein, no reliable instrument was used to measure suicidal ideation or attempt. They were all based from client self-reports and they were not validated from other sources. In short, the weakness of this study lies in the reliability (or lack of it) of the research instruments used. Therapist variables such as accuracy in recording the abuse and suicide history, willingness to listen and to help, work load, and the kind of relationship between the therapist and the client, are also important factors to look into as they would affect the integrity of the data used.

Although this study targeted specifically rural mental health patients, it did not illustrate any significant findings that would pertain specifically to this sample. The results of this study support previous findings of other studies that childhood sexual abuse is a significant risk factor for suicidal behavior in adulthood. It appears that the link between childhood abuse and adult suicidal behavior cuts across geographic locations and the association can be found regardless of geographic region. Since the prevalence of mental health problems among rural and urban adult populations are similar (National Rural Health Association, 1999), more research on rural mental health needs and services should be conducted. Doing so will ensure a more adequate, effective, and culturally competent practice with rural populations. The design and delivery of rural mental health services requires a unique set of knowledge, skills, and abilities because rural areas in the United States are geographically and culturally diverse (Sawyer & Beeson, 1998).

It is recommended that future research use more reliable instruments to measure abuse and suicide histories. Future research should also examine the influence of abuse severity on adult suicidal behavior, use a more diverse sample, and collect data using multiple instruments. Since this study did not look into causation but only the correlation between adult suicidal behavior and childhood abuse, future studies can use other statistical tests to predict the likelihood of adult suicide based from the different types of childhood abuse.

CONCLUSION

Since adults who had been victims of childhood abuse utilize healthcare services for mental health problems, a history of childhood abuse should be part of the protocol in order to assess potential for suicidality. A routine psychosocial history that includes history of child abuse will help mental health care workers in assessing the risk factors for suicidality among people that utilize mental health services in the community. Childhood abuse is a risk factor for suicide and its early identification is necessary in suicide prevention. Early identification, accurate assessment, and prevention are essential for suicide prevention. Moreover, a preventive rather than a reactive approach to this problem is more cost efficient. Although risk factors such as childhood abuse are not necessarily causes of suicide in adulthood (DHHS, 2005), reducing the risk factors, and enhancing protective factors such as having an effective and easy access to mental health services and effective clinical care will greatly reduce the risks associated with suicide. More research on rural mental health needs and adequacy of mental health services should be conducted in order determine the unique needs of people in rural areas and come up with an adequate, effective, and culturally competent mental health practice.

REFERENCES

American Psychological Association (1995). *Rural health in America*. Retrieved November 19, 2002, from http://www.apa.org/practice/rural.html

Anderson, P., Tiro, J., Price, A., Bender, M., & Kaslow, N. (2002). Additive impact of childhood emotional, physical, and sexual abuse on suicide attempts among low-income African American women. *Suicide and Life-Threatening Behavior, 32*(2), 131-138.

Barker-Collo, S. (2001). Adult reports of child and adult attributions of blame for child sexual abuse: Predicting adult adjustment and suicidal behaviors in females. *Child Abuse and Neglect, 25*(10), 1329-1341.

Beck, A., Steer, R., Beck, J., & Newman, C. (1993). Hopelessness, depression, suicidal ideation, and clinical diagnosis of depression. *Suicide and Life-Threatening Behavior, 23*(2), 139-145.

Briere, J., & Runtz, M. (1986). Suicidal thoughts and behavior in former sexual abuse victims. *Canadian journal of Behavioural Science, 18*(4), 413-423.

Brown, A., & Finkelhor, D. (1986). Impact of child sexual abuse: A review of the research. *Psychological Bulletin, 99*(1), 66-77.

Brown, J., Cohen, P., Johnson, J., & Smailes, E. (1999). Childhood abuse and neglect: Specificity of effects on adolescent and young adult depression and suicidality. *Journal of the American Academy of Child and Adolescent Psychiatry, 38*(12), 1490-1496.

Bryant, S., & Range, L. (1995). Suicidality in college women who report multiple versus single types of maltreatment by parents: A brief report. *Journal of Child Sexual Abuse, 4*(3), 87-95.

Centers for Disease Control and Prevention. (1998). CDC Surveillance Summaries, August 14, 1998. *Morbidity and Mortality Weekly Report, 47*, 41-49.

Centers for Disease Control and Prevention, National Center for Injury Prevention and Control (2004). *Web-based Injury Statistics Query and Reporting System (WISQARS)*. Retrieved June 30, 2005, from http://www.cdc.gov/ncipc/wisqars/default.htm

Centers for Disease Control and Prevention, National Center for Injury Prevention and Control (2005). *Suicide: Fact sheet.* Retrieved June 30, 2005, from http://www. cdc.gov/ncipc/factsheets/suifacts.htm

Conner, K., Duberstein, P., Conwell, Y., Seidlitz, L., & Caine, E. (2001). Psychological vulnerability to completed suicide: A review of empirical studies. *Suicide and Life-Threatening Behavior, 31*(4), 367-385.

Davidson, J., Hughes, D., George, L., & Blazer, D. (1996). The association of sexual assault and attempted suicide within the community. *Archives of General Psychiatry, 53,* 550-555.

Dube, S., Anda, R., Felitti, V., Chapman, D., Wiliamson, D., & Giles, W. (2001). Childhood abuse, household dysfunction, and the risk of attempted suicide throughout the life span. *The Journal of the American Medical Association, 286*(24), 3089-3096.

Ernst, C., Angst, J., & Foldenyi, M. (1993). The Zurich study XVII. Sexual abuse in childhood. Frequency and relevance for adult morbidity: Data of a longitudinal epidemiological study. *European Archives of Psychiatry and Clinical Neuroscience, 242*(5), 293-300.

Farber, E., Herbert, S., & Reviere, S. (1996). Childhood abuse and suicidality in obstetrics patients in a hospital-based urban prenatal clinic. *General Hospital Psychiatry, 18,* 56-60.

Garno, J., Goldberg, J., Ramirez, M., & Ritzler, B. (2005). Impact of childhood abuse on the clinical course of bipolar disorder. *British Journal of Psychiatry, 186,* 121-125.

Gibb, B., Alloy, L., Abramson, L., Rose, D., Whitehouse, W., & Hogan, M. (2001). Child maltreatment and college students' current suicidal ideation: A test of the hopelessness theory. *Suicide and Life-Threatening Behavior, 31*(4), 405-415.

Katerndahl, D., Burge, S., & Kellogg, N. (2005). Predictors of development of adult psychopathology in female victims of childhood sexual abuse. *The Journal of Nervous and Mental Disease, 193*(4), 258-264.

Kessler, R., Borges, G., & Walters, E. (1999). Prevalence of and risk factors for lifetime suicide attempts in the national comorbidity survey. *Archives of General Psychiatry, 56,* 617-626.

Lundqvist, G., Svedin, G., & Hansson, K. (2004). Childhood sexual abuse. Women's health when starting in group therapy. *Nordic Journal of Psychiatry, 58*(1), 25-32.

McCauley, J., Kern, D., Kolodner, K., Dill, L., Schroeder, A., & DeChant, H. et al. (1997). Clinical characteristics of women with a history of childhood abuse. *The Journal of the American Medical Association, 277*(17), 1362-1368.

McHolm, A., MacMillan, H., & Jamieson, E. (2003). The relationship between childhood physical abuse and suicidality among depressed women: Results from a community sample. *American Journal of Psychiatry, 160*(5), 933-938.

Molnar, B., Buka, S., & Kessler, R. (2001). Child sexual abuse and subsequent psychopathology: Results from the National Comorbidity Survey. *American Journal of Public Health, 91*(5), 753-760.

Molnar, B., Berkman, L., & Buka, S. (2001). Psychopathology, childhood sexual abuse and other childhood adversities: Relative links to subsequent suicidal behaviour in the US. *Psychological Medicine, 31*(6), 965-977.

National Center for Health Statistics. (2004). *National vital statistics reports.* Retrieved September 1, 2004, from http://www.cdc.gov

National Rural Health Association. (1999). *Mental Health in Rural America.* Retrieved November 19, 2002, from http://www.nrharural.org/dc/issuepapers/ipaper14.html

Nilsen, W., & Conner, K. (2002). The association between suicidal ideation and childhood and adult victimization. *Journal of Child Sexual Abuse, 11*(3), 49-62.

Oquendo, M., Brent, D., Birmaher, B., Greenhill, L., Kolko, D., & Stanley, B. et al. (2005). Posttraumatic stress disorder comorbid with major depression: Factors mediating the association with suicidal behavior. *American Journal of Psychiatry, 162*(3), 560-566.

Osvath, P., Voros, V., & Fekete, S. (2004). Life events and psychopathology in a group of suicide attempters. *Psychopathology, 37*(1), 36-40.

Peters, D., & Range, L. (1995). Childhood sexual abuse and current suicidality in college women and men. *Child Abuse and Neglect, 19*(3), 335-341.

Read, J., Agar, K., Barker-Collo, S., Davies, E., & Moskowitz, A. (2001). Assessing suicidality in adults: Integrating childhood trauma as a major risk factor. *Professional Psychology: Research and Practice, 32*(4), 367-372.

Rind, B., Tromovitch, P., & Bauserman, R. (1998). A meta-analytic examination of assumed properties of child sexual abuse using college samples. *Psychological Bulletin, 126*, 22-52.

Rossow, I., & Lauritzen, G. (2001). Shattered childhood: A key issue in suicidal behavior among drug addicts? *Addiction, 96*(2), 227-240.

Roy, A. (2001a). Childhood trauma and suicidal behavior in male cocaine dependent patients. *Suicide and Life-Threatening Behavior, 31*(2), 194-196.

Roy, A. (2001b). Childhood trauma and hostility as an adult: Relevance to suicidal behavior. *Psychiatry Research, 102*, 97-101.

Roy, A. (2004). Relationship of childhood trauma to age of first suicide attempt and number of attempts in substance dependent patients. *Acta Psychiatrica Scandinavica, 109*(2), 121-125.

Santa Mina, E., & Gallop, R. (1998). Childhood sexual and physical abuse and adult self-harm and suicidal behaviour: A literature review. *Canadian Journal of Psychiatry, 43*(8), 793-800.

Sawyer, D., & Beeson, P. (1998). *Rural mental health: Vision 2000 and beyond.* Retrieved November 19, 2002, from http://www.narmh.org/pages/future.html

Soloff, P., Lynch, K., & Kelly, T. (2002). Childhood abuse as a risk factor for suicidal behavior in borderline personality disorder. *Journal of Personality Disorder, 16*(3), 201-214.

Stepakoff, S. (1998). Effects of sexual victimization on suicidal ideation and behavior in US college women. *Suicide and Life-Threatening Behavior, 28*(1), 107-126.

Thakkar, R., Gutierrez, P., Kuczen, C., & McCanne, T. (2000). History of physical and/or sexual abuse and current suicidality in college women. *Child Abuse and Neglect, 24*(10), 1345-1354.

Ullman, S., & Brecklin, L. (2002). Sexual assault history and suicidal behavior in a national sample of women. *Suicide and Life-Threatening Behavior, 32*(2), 117-130.

U.S. Department of Health and Human Services. (2005). *The Surgeon General's Call to Action to Prevent Suicide, 1999.* Retrieved June 30, 2005, from http://www.surgeongeneral.gov/library/calltoaction/fact1.htm

Whiffen, V., & MacIntosh, H. (2005). Mediators of the link between childhood sexual abuse and emotional distress. *Trauma, Violence, and Abuse, 6*(1), 24-39.

Yang, B., & Clum, G. (2000). Childhood stress leads to later suicidality via its effect on cognitive functioning. *Suicide and Life-Threatening Behavior, 30*(3), 183-198.

Ystgaard, M., Hestetun, I., Loeb, M., & Mehlum, L. (2004). Is there a specific relationship between childhood sexual and physical abuse and repeated suicidal behavior? *Child Abuse and Neglect, 28*, 863-875.

doi:10.1300/J394v04n01_05

The Effectiveness
of Court-Mandated Treatment
on Recidivism Among Juvenile Offenders

Leia Farrouki
Andridia V. Mapson, MSW

SUMMARY. This article presents the results of a study that looked at the effectiveness of court-mandated treatment on recidivism among juvenile offenders. Archival data was used to look at a sample of 100 juveniles who had participated in court-mandated treatment. Logistic regression analysis was used to analyze the posttest only design data with no control groups. Results showed that there were significant differences in reported recidivism by those who completed court-mandated treatment versus those who did not successfully complete treatment. Court-mandated treatment was statistically significant in determining whether a juvenile offender reoffends. Future research should look at variables that may contribute to the rise in delinquency. It is imperative that service delivery professionals receive adequate training and educational opportunities to become more knowledgeable about delinquency. The lack of training can lead to ineffective treatment approaches and the potential for further harm and incarceration of adolescents. doi:10.1300/ J394v04n01_06 *[Article copies available for a fee from The Haworth Document Delivery Service: 1-800-HAWORTH. E-mail address: <docdelivery@haworthpress.com>*

Leia Farrouki and Andridia V. Mapson are affiliated with The University of Tennessee, College of Social Work, 303 Henson Hall, Knoxville, TN 37996 (E-mail: avmapson@hotmail.com).

[Haworth co-indexing entry note]: "The Effectiveness of Court-Mandated Treatment on Recidivism Among Juvenile Offenders." Farrouki, Leia, and Andridia V. Mapson. Co-published simultaneously in *Journal of Evidence-Based Social Work* (The Haworth Press, Inc.) Vol. 4, No. 1/2, 2007, pp. 79-95; and: *Building Excellence: The Rewards and Challenges of Integrating Research into the Undergraduate Curriculum* (ed: Catherine N. Dulmus, and Karen M. Sowers) The Haworth Press, 2007, pp. 79-95. Single or multiple copies of this article are available for a fee from The Haworth Document Delivery Service [1-800-HAWORTH, 9:00 a.m. - 5:00 p.m. (EST). E-mail address: docdelivery@haworthpress.com].

Available online at http://jebsw.haworthpress.com
doi:10.1300/J394v04n01_06

KEYWORDS. Juvenile offenders, court-mandated treatment, recidivism

INTRODUCTION

Juvenile crime has been a problem for the past hundred years. The number of adolescents being incarcerated and otherwise involved in the juvenile justice system in the United States has continued to rise over the past decade. There has also been a trend of increased violent offending among adolescents, especially females. These trends have caused alarm in the public during the past decade and challenged the juvenile justice system. The increases in delinquency over the past decade are rooted in a number of social problems (i.e., family fragmentation, child abuse, alcohol and drug abuse, adolescent conflict, and early sexual involvement) that may originate from the family structure. Many incarcerated adolescents have behavioral and emotional problems that would quality them for treatment programs.

Criminal behavior committed by juveniles involves all types of offenses and is committed by juveniles from all backgrounds, cultures, ethnicity, races, and religions. Due to the myriad crimes juveniles can commit, legal officials divide delinquent acts into two categories. The first is a status offense, which is defined as conduct, which would not, under law, be an offense if committed by an adult such as truancy, running away, or underage drinking (Calhoun, Jurgens, and Chen (1993). The second category is index offenses. The Juvenile Detention and Correctional Facility Census (1987) classified various index offenses and placed them in categories according to degree of severity: (1) Violent crimes such as murder, rape, robbery, and aggravated assault, and (2) property crimes such as arson, motor-vehicle theft, and burglary.

This paper will evaluate the effectiveness of court-mandated treatment for juvenile offenders by looking at past literature and the recidivism rates of those juveniles who were involved in a treatment program. Re-offending will be defined as someone who has completed a combination of the programs or probation and after they turn eighteen, commits a crime of equal or greater status.

LITERATURE REVIEW

It is necessary to review previous literature on juvenile delinquency, risk and protective factors, school prevention programs, interventions for delinquency, recidivism rates, and efficacy of treatment programs to gain an understanding regarding the effects and benefits of court mandated treatment for juvenile delinquents, which may offer an explanation for the decrease or increase in recidivism after release.

Juvenile Delinquency

Juvenile delinquency is defined as an adolescent under the age of eighteen that is apprehended my law officials for committing a crime, and found guilty by a judge for committing the act (Calhoun, Jurgens, & Chen, 1993). Thornberry, Huizinga, and Loeber (2004) stated "although the U.S. delinquency rate has declined since the mid-1990's, it is still among the highest in the industrialized countries and it is essential to develop effective intervention programs, which depends on a firm, scientific understanding of the origins of delinquency" (p. 3). This study consists of three longitudinal studies with samples representing the broader population of urban adolescents. The Denver Youth Survey was used which is based upon "a probability sample of households in high-risk neighborhoods of Denver, CO, selected on the basis of their population, housing characteristics, and high official crime rates" (Thornberry et al., 2004, p. 3). The survey respondents included 1,527 children ages 7-15 in 1987 and who lived in one of the 20,000 randomly selected households.

The Pittsburgh Youth study was based on a sample of 1,517 boys from Pittsburgh, PA in 1987-88. To identify high-risk participants, a screening assessment was conducted of problem behaviors in the first, fourth, and seventh grades in the Pittsburgh public school system. The Rochester Youth Development study was based on a sample of 729 boys and 271 girls in the seventh and eighth grades in public schools of Rochester, NY, in 1988 (Thornberry et al., 2004). Collectively, these studies provide data on delinquent behavior from 1987 to present and have more than 4,000 participants ranging in age from 7 to 30. The key topics covered were childhood aggression, developmental pathways to delinquency, and the overlap of problem behaviors. The studies provide descriptive data that trace the onset and development of delinquency (Thornberry et al., 2004).

The strengths of this study are that it is the largest, comprehensive investigation of the causes and correlates of delinquency (Thornberry et al., 2004). It included a sample of 20,000 households. A limitation of this study is that it does not address the effects of programs on recidivism rates. Another limitation is that many youth who commit serious offenses experience difficulties in other areas of life, with the exception of drug use, but little is known about the overlap of these problem behaviors in the general populations (Thornberry et al., 2004). There are a number of offenders entering the juvenile justice system who have drug, alcohol, school or mental health-related problems but are not receiving any treatment in the community or while incarcerated.

Risk and Protective Factors Related to Juvenile Delinquency

Reducing delinquency and youth violence is the main goal of the Title V program. New York's Delinquency Prevention Program focuses on risk and protective factors that were proved to be related to juvenile delinquency. By using this approach, communities can identify the risk factors that contribute to delinquency problems. Risk factors include: alcohol and drug use; long-term unemployment; poor academic achievement; truancy; negative peer influence, and high levels of community violence (Juvenile Delinquency Prevention Program Fact Sheet, 2004).

An article from the New York State juvenile delinquency program discussed the risk and protective factors related to juvenile delinquency. Once the risk factors were determined (i.e., drug use, truancy, etc.), the community increases the protective factors (i.e., mentoring programs, organized family activities, academic tutoring) that can prevent or reduce delinquent behaviors. The main concept is that preventing delinquent behavior is more cost efficient than rehabilitation. However, the "costs" are measurable in money and lives. This program considers the influence of family, peer group, school, and the community on a child's development. The communities must provide intervention and/or prevention programs depending on their specific characteristics and needs (Juvenile Delinquency Prevention Program Fact Sheet, 2004).

School Prevention Programs

This section will discuss the effectiveness of violence prevention programs in schools, which is important because of the age of the participants and the fact that violence is a prevalent offense among juvenile delinquents. The effective treatment options described in these articles could prove to be very important to juvenile delinquent research.

According to a comprehensive study conducted by Griffin et al. (2002), whole school interventions are more successful in reducing violence than programs aiming at specific groups. The study also found that alternative schools or programs are the least successful. However, when these were compared to comparison schools, all of the programs studied showed some success in deterring victimization and perpetration. Griffin et al. (2002), noted, "this is the optimal approach to combat violence against African-American middle school kids. They have different experiences than suburban kids might. You have to tailor the intervention to the population" (Varied Violence, 2002). The fact that the schools involved in this study have 99% African-American populations is strength to this study, proving that interventions do in fact, depend on the individual. However, it is a weakness because not only does the population usually studied consist of a very low percentage of African-Americans, the current study will not be inclusive of only one particular population.

Another article also discusses the effectiveness of school-based violence prevention programs. School violence has a significant impact on student and teachers. Forty-three of every thousand children were victims of nonfatal violent crimes at school or on their way to or from school and more than 250,000 serious crimes such as rape and assault were reported. Thirty-one of every thousand teachers were victimized (Miller, 2003). Miller (2003) conducted a meta-analysis were studies were found through a systematic review of electronic databases and bibliographies. The settings included elementary, middle, and high schools and it targets children identified as high risk for aggressive behavior. Forty-four studies were located but none reported data on violent injuries. In the 28 trials that reported aggressive behavior, those who were in the intervention group showed a greater reduction of aggressive behavior than those in the nonintervention group. Aggressive behavior was also reduced when schools or agencies responded to aggressive behavior.

The analysis found that interventions were more effective when administered to older children and to mixed sex groups rather than boys alone. A limitation to this study is that it used a small sample and the authors stress the need to have results confirmed by large, high-quality trials. It is concluded that the school-based prevention programs may reduce violent and aggressive behaviors in children who already exhibit a tendency toward such behaviors (Miller, 2003).

The last article describes the implementation of a collaborative preventive intervention project designed to reduce the levels of bullying and other related antisocial behavior among children attending two urban middle schools with primarily African-American students enrolled. These schools have high rates or juvenile violence reflected by suspensions and expulsions for behavioral problems. An empirically based drug and violence prevention program, Bullying Prevention and Project ALERT were implemented into each middle school. An intensive evidence-based intervention and multisystemic therapy (MST) were also used to target students at risk of expulsion and court referral (Cunningham & Henggeler, 2001).

The goals of this project include reduced youth violence, reduced drug use, and improved psychosocial functioning of the participating youth. A quasi-experimental design was used to determine the combined effects of the prevention and intervention programs. Following the collection of baseline data during the first year, schools were randomly assigned to either experimental or controlled conditions during year two. By the third year, intervention and prevention programs were delivered in both middle schools. Two sets of measures were gathered. One pertains to the outcomes that examine the effects of the school-wide bullying and drug prevention programs and the second pertains to the outcomes achieved by MST (Cunningham & Henggeler, 2001). All the programs (i.e., Prevention: Bullying Prevention program, Project ALERT) and intervention (i.e., MST) have been proven to be effective but when combined, they perform at an optimal level and address known risk factors for antisocial behavior while building protective factors. A limitation to the study is that the design did not have best internal validity (Cunningham & Henggeler, 2001).

Interventions for Delinquency

A review of criminological and psychiatric outcome literature was conducted focusing on psychosocial interventions for delinquency as well as responses by the juvenile justice system. It includes studies on the effectiveness of interventions for delinquency that were in a comparison or control setting with large sample sizes. This review discusses traditional and innovative approaches. The innovative approaches include rehabilitative and community-based programs. The review also discusses educational programs and meta-analyses of psychosocial treatments for delinquency. Another section of the review discusses the standard psychosocial approaches and multi-systemic therapy (MST)

(Kurtz, 2002). Multi-systemic therapy has been shown to reduce offending rates. It is based on an assessment of factors contributing to each individual's offending behavior, and aims to create change at the individual, family, school, and community level using family and behavioral therapy. Kurtz (2002) attempts to review, many of the different approaches to juvenile delinquency intervention and treatment. His review shows the ineffectiveness of probation programs and one study proved again the negative outcome of punitive approaches. The review also points out the link between delinquency and school performance. The results found that alternative education programs had small positive effects on self-esteem and school-related variables, but did not have any significant improvement in delinquent activity (Kurtz, 2002).

Efficacy of Treatment Programs

Group home treatment is one of the oldest options in treatment for juvenile offenders providing a family-type atmosphere that studies show has a significant impact on the recidivism rates among this population, especially among first-time offenders. Haghighi and Lopez (1993) conducted an empirical study on the success or failure of group home treatment programs for juveniles. The authors point out that, "recently group home treatment programs have come under criticism … because some believe that group home treatment programs … have failed to produce a significant difference in the overall rate of delinquency" (p. 2). During a 2-year period (1988-1990), 410 juveniles were referred to group home treatment in a midwestern state. The intake reflected 304 referrals and of the 304 referrals, 152 residents were randomly selected for analysis. A majority of the residents were referred to group home treatment subsequent to unsatisfactory results from probation, detention, and other alternatives. Juvenile backgrounds and their dispositions as to type of treatment are compared so that suggestions can be made for the most effective treatment in reducing the recidivism rate.

Haghighi and Lopez (1993) report that the interruption of delinquent behavior is what indicates the success or failure of a program. The results showed that of the 152 cases, 95 (62.5%) successfully completed the group home treatment program and did not reappear in the juvenile court system until the age of 18. Fifty-seven (37.5%) of the cases failed the program reflecting they committed a delinquent act subsequent to release from the group home treatment. The sample included 31 girls and 121 boys. The analysis revealed that the success or failure of the group home program depends on when the juveniles were referred to the treatment program. The program was most successful when delin-quent children were referred in the early stages of delinquency. It was least effective after the commission of the fourth delinquent act.

A study conducted by Quinn and Van Dyke (2004) compares recidi-vism rates among those who completed the multiple-family group-intervention program (MFGI), the Family Solutions Program, to two other groups of first-time juvenile offenders. The article discusses the need for effective interventions with juvenile delinquents and places importance, by empirical evidence, for the need of family inclusion in treatment. The authors point out that "currently there are no major stud-ies examining or demonstrating effective intervention with juvenile *first-time* offenders" (Quinn & Van Dyke, 2004, p. 179).

Four hundred and fifty-five first-time juvenile offenders and their parents participated in the study. They came from two counties in Northeast Georgia. The sampling for the study was a convenience sam-ple from extant data from 1993 to 2001 for MFGI and probation. Due to non-random assignment to treatment, the group demographics were dif-ferent, especially the racial makeup of probation (majority Caucasian) compared to the intervention (majority African American). Ethnicity was used as a covariate in every analysis because of this difference (Quinn & Van Dyke, 2004). The total number of participants referred to FSP was 360 but the graduates of FSP consisted of 267 participants, while 93 dropped out. An initial comparison group of 107 adolescents received probation in a different county in which first-offender youths were re-ferred to FSP. This was also a convenience sample. The total number of youth in the probation group was 95 youth for comparison analysis. Twelve youth did not complete their probation requirements (Quinn & Van Dyke, 2004).

Using logistic regression analysis, the study found that first time offenders placed on probation were 9.3 times more likely to re-offend compared to the Family Solutions Program (FSP) graduates. Families referred to FSP but who dropped out was 4.4 times more likely to re-offend compared to FSP graduates. An intent-to-treat model comparing the combined group of FSP graduates and dropouts with the probation group indicated that youth in the probation group were 8.1 times more likely to re-offend than youth referred to FSP (Quinn & Van Dyke, 2004). Results indicated better outcomes on recidivism for those who completed FSP for both male and female youth. A study by Lipsey & Wilson (1998) stated, "probation had a weak or no effect in reducing re-cidivism of serious offenders [because] the most effective interventions involved family, individual behaviors and cognition, and community."

The study claims that probation is merely punitive and does not focus on positive alternatives.

Research conducted on the effectiveness of counseling services on adjudicated delinquent youths compares the recidivism rates of the youth who received counseling services with the rates of a control group that had not received any counseling services (Kadish, Glaser, Calhoun & Risler, 1999). The Juvenile Counseling and Assessment Program (JCAP) strives to assist delinquents in dealing with "the complex difficulties that they face in their lives to improve their social skills, to make them aware of their own and their community's resources and to ultimately reduce the likelihood that they will become further involved in the legal system" (Kadish et al., 1999, p. 2).

Data was gathered from juvenile court records and a six-month follow-up after the termination of counseling, the researchers counted the number of re-offenses that each of the juveniles committed. Kadish et al. (1999) question whether counseling can be effective in producing change among delinquents. The findings supported the hypothesis in that only 25% of the juveniles who went through JCAP re-offended compared to 64% of the juveniles who received regular probation services re-offended. This research shows that a combination of approaches is effective in addressing the complexity of problems associated with juvenile delinquents. It also concludes that the family is the most important system in youth's lives and therefore change will come when youth are worked with in the context of their families, schools and communities (Kadish et al., 1999).

There were several limitations to the study, which include the fact that the study used an unequal control group design, which made the selection process a threat to the internal validity of the study. Those who received counseling may have had some trait that influenced the probation officer to refer them to counseling. It was not possible to use a controlled experimental design due to restrictions on the particular setting used. Furthermore, the juveniles in the group who did not participate in JCAP could have received other counseling services unknown to the researcher that may have influenced their outcome.

Impact of Restitution

Roy (1995) examines the impact of restitution on recidivism rates. It is believed that paying restitution itself is rehabilitative, however it discusses the on-going debate as to whether restitution actually reduces recidivism. This study discusses a restitution program in Lake County,

Indiana. It relays the importance recidivism plays in the effectiveness of programs. It is pointed out that few studies have been done in privately operated juvenile programs. The researcher states that "the sentencing goal of restitution is to promote an increased sense of accountability and responsibility leading to reduced offender recidivism" (Roy, 1995, p. 2). It allows justice to be achieved while offenders are perceived as responsible. It points out that the limitations in research is that it doesn't look at whether or not the restitution programs reduced offender recidivism, therefore this study examines the hypothesis that there was no significant difference in recidivism between the juveniles sentenced to probation-only or restitution. This is a very important aspect and it is believed the program would show a reduction in recidivism rates among first-time offenders (Roy, 1995).

The participants in the "restitution" group were 113 juveniles who were successful in the program from 1989-1990 and the "probation only" group consisted of 148 youths. Both groups were followed through the end of 1992 for recidivism reports. The dependent variable "recidivism" was measured in terms of number and types of offenses as well as reconviction of the successful participants during follow-up. The independent variables included individual characteristics (i.e., race, gender, age), case characteristics (i.e., prior offense, substance abuse history, prior detention), and a program characteristic (i.e., number of days in program supervision) (Roy, 1995).

Overall, 113 participants in the "restitution" group and 148 in the "probation only" group completed their program requirements. Both groups included first-time as well as repeat offenders. Thirty-six of the youth in the "restitution" group and 64 juveniles in the "probation only" group were reconvicted for new offenses. In regard to first-time offenders, 20 of them in the "restitution" group and 22 in the "probation only" group were reconvicted. As far as repeat offenders, in both groups, 50% were reconvicted.

The literature review defends the theory that many different approaches to reducing juvenile delinquency are effective. Recidivism rates were used to determine the effectiveness of each program, as will be used to determine the effectiveness of the programs being studied. As noted earlier, intervention really depends upon the individual in need, however, these studies show which programs are proved to be the most effective. The following research will show whether or not two specific court-mandated programs are effective in reducing the recidivism rate among juvenile delinquents. The literature shows that most programs, if implemented correctly, will have some degree of a positive effect on the population they are serving. The literature also shows prevention proves to be the most effective tool for deterring delinquency and court referrals.

Research Question

The research question for the current study is:

1. What factors predict treatment outcomes and criminal recidivism in a sample of status and delinquent juvenile offenders participating in court-mandated programs?

METHODOLOGY

Sample

The sample consisted of 100 juveniles who have completed a court-mandated treatment program or who have turned eighteen years of age, which means they are no longer part of the juvenile system. Juveniles were randomly selected from one court system. Fifty juveniles were from Program A (status offenders) and 50 from Program B (delinquent offenders). The Juvenile Court has jurisdiction over them until they turn age 19 or until they finish the program. If the juvenile is charged with being ungovernable, the jurisdiction stops at age 18 because unruly/ungovernable behavior is a status offense, not something you can be charged with as an adult. However, if the juvenile was a delinquent and he or she turns 18 years old while on probation, they would continue to remain on probation. If they receive a new charge against them, for example Driving Under the Influence (DUI), they would be tried as an adult in general sessions court, or criminal Court, depending on the charge.

Sample characteristics include Gender: 70 Male (70%), 30 Female (30%); Ethnicity: 83 Caucasian (83%); 17 other (17%). Mean Age: 16.05 (S.D. = 0.989); Has a Prior Juvenile Offense Record: 61 (61%); Successful Completion of Treatment: 77 (77%) and Re-offends after Treatment: 30 (30%)

Files of juveniles who entered the court when they were of age 13 and who have turned 18 were specifically looked at to monitor the recidivism rate between those ages. The decision to evaluate these programs with those terms was due to these programs being responsible for the juvenile's actions while they remain juveniles. The juvenile system cannot be held accountable for their actions once they are adults. One of the best ways to prove the effectiveness of these court-mandated programs will be to use closed cases. There are many combinations of programs the juveniles participate in based on the severity of their offense and their previous record.

First time offenders with charges such as truancy, being ungovernable, or possession of tobacco products may be placed under the supervision of the court or be required to complete a specific program depending on their need. If court staff determines that the juvenile needs a more strict probation, they will be placed on state probation with the Department of Children Services (DCS). If the severity of the offense is even higher, the juvenile has the opportunity to go through intensive probation with a treatment program, which is their last resort before going into state custody. In order to be placed in a treatment program, the child must be committable and must be assessed or evaluated by the Department of Children Services *Risk Score Analysis*. They must rate a score that would be sufficient to be committed to the custody of the state. Furthermore, the Judge will make a determination that a prospective youth is appropriate and that he/she and his/her parent are committed to participating and cooperating in the intensive probation program. The treatment program also accepts youth that are currently in DCS custody who are incarcerated in a department institution or group home.

Under any of these probation requirements, part of the court order could include participation in another program. The second program is a character education intervention program specifically designed to meet the needs of the older and at-risk youth. The program consists of six two hour sessions focusing on character education, self-exploration and ethical decision making activities that have proven effective with older youth's and teenagers. The juveniles must complete the six sessions, do all necessary homework and volunteer activities in order to graduate from the program. The juveniles are referred to this program by the schools, courts and social service agencies in hopes that the involvement will make a difference in keeping them out of trouble and out of the legal system.

The sampling plan used was one of convenience ensuring 50 files were obtained from those that have participated in each program. In order to insure a consistent sample for the study, recent files were selected and from those selected, every third file was used to complete the research study. If the third file happened not to fall in either of the categories stated, the fifth file was selected and so on. Both the treatment program and education intervention program were evaluated in the study. The research question will be answered by looking at the files relevant to research and than searching public records to see if the files chosen have adult records. This will determine if court-mandated treatment is effective by obtaining recidivism rates.

Data Collection

Data for the study were collected from a southeast court system. Archival data collected at this site were used as well as juvenile court employees because they also had information about the clients who have come through the court system. Some disadvantages or limitations of the study site were human error or typographical errors, the fact that the records might not be recent and up-to-date or not enough of the same combination of programs to prove its effectiveness.

Files were selected from closed cases in the juvenile court as well. In order to insure the sampling procedure was consistent, every third file was used. Files were read and relevant information was recorded. All of the files contained most of the following information: court orders, social history, medical/psychiatric evaluations, petitions, court recordings, police reports, program evaluations and discharge, a recent photo and identifying information. The Judge, probation officers, secretaries, case managers and the doctors who have performed evaluations wrote and placed this information in the files. Some limitations that may be encountered are that the files could be inconsistent or missing information if a participant was not asked all of the questions. Consent from the study was obtained from the juvenile court and data collected was unidentifiable and cannot be traced back to the juvenile participants, as participants' names were not recorded. Also, all juvenile matters, especially their court hearings, are closed to the public. The dependent variable will be re-offending as adults and the independent variable will be participation in court-mandated treatment.

DATA ANALYSIS

Posttest only design was used with no control groups for the study. The sample was one of convenience. Frequency distributions were computed for each of the demographic and study variables to complete a profile analysis of the sample. Logistic regression was used to analyze the data and assess whether court-mandated treatment had an effect on recidivism rates and if completing the court-mandated treatment had an effect on recidivism rates as well. The two logistic regression models were: No Re-Offending after Treatment (coded as 1; Re-offending coded as 0) Successful Completion of Treatment (coded as 1; Unsuccessful Completion coded as 0). A comparison was made between two of the more widely used programs to evaluate their effectiveness. It is hoped that court-mandated programs are effective in reducing the recidivism rate. The treatment program has a six-month follow up evaluation, which was utilized in the study.

RESULTS

There were significant differences in reported recidivism by those who completed court-mandated treatment versus those who did not successfully complete treatment. The results indicated that 30% of juveniles re-offended after treatment and juveniles who successfully complete treatment are 22.1 times more likely to not re-offend than those who did not successfully complete treatment. Juveniles with a prior juvenile offense are 82.4% more likely to not successfully complete treatment than those without a prior juvenile offense. Out of 30 juveniles predicted to reoffend, 12 did who completed court-mandated treatment and 18 that didn't complete court-mandated treatment reoffended. Out of 70 juveniles, those who completed court-mandated treatment, 65 did not reoffend and 5 that didn't complete court-mandated treatment did not reoffend. Court-mandated treatment was statistically significant in determining whether a juvenile offender reoffends. When gender and race was added into the regression model, there was no difference in whether a person reoffended. Gender or race makes no difference, only court-mandated treatment. When looking at the prior offense variable, those

MODEL I. No Re-Offending After Treatment

Independent Variable	B	Significance	Exp (B)
Male	−0.576	.367	0.562
Age in Years	0.183	.511	1.201
Caucasian	−0.836	.304	0.433
Enrolled in Program B	0.377	.597	1.458
Prior Juvenile Offense Record	0.067	.930	1.069
Successful Completion of Treatment	3.096	.001	22.101

Model X^2 = 34.17, df = 6, p < .001; No Future Re-offending coded as 1; Future Re-offending coded as 0

MODEL II. Successful Completion of Treatment

Independent Variable	B	Significance	Exp (B)
Male	−0.706	.279	0.494
Age in Years	0.493	.051	1.638
Caucasian	0.276	.671	1.318
Enrolled in Program B	0.286	.649	1.332
Prior Juvenile Offense	−1.737	.028	.176
Constant	−5.243	.213	.005

Model X^2 = 15.44, df = 5, p = .009; Successful Completion coded as 1; Unsuccessful completion coded as 0.

with no prior offense, 30 of the 39 didn't reoffend and 9 did reoffend. Those with a prior offense, 40 of the 61 did not reoffend and 21 did reoffend. When added into the regression model, prior offense made no difference in whether a juvenile reoffended or not, court-mandated treatment is the only significant factor in recidivism rates. Model 1 and Model II displays the logistic regression analysis.

DISCUSSION

Despite the widespread concern regarding crime and violence, public support for court-mandated treatment has never been a priority. This is due, in part, to society's lack of sympathy for this population and a resulting punitive attitude. A reason for this attitude is the public's perception that not only is treatment questionable, but those who do not respond well to treatment are "beyond hope." Given this view, some feel investing in multiple treatments is a waste of money. Stiffer sentences and more juvenile cells are more tangible than a promise of treatment cure.

The purpose of this study was to determine if court-mandated treatment was effective in reducing recidivism among juvenile offenders. Effective treatment is crucial in preventing recidivism among juvenile offenders. The results showed that court-mandated treatment was the only variable significant in reducing recidivism among offenders. When looking at gender, race, sex, and prior offense, those variables had no effect on whether an individual reoffended or not. Some limitations of the data include limited ethnic diversity, administrative data and data from one court system.

But, this is only one study looking at a limited population. At a minimum, these findings must be confirmed. To do this, we need to re-examine prior results in this context and design future studies so they can take into account previous treatment history as well as the impact of the current treatment. These limitations not withstanding, what the results do suggest is important: Treatment may be a cumulative process with each treatment either making a person more susceptible to treatment or actually reducing further criminal activity.

IMPLICATIONS FOR SOCIAL WORK PRACTICE

The juvenile justice system has acted as a dynamic system that has many ailments. Therefore, the juvenile justice system needs to be continuously challenged to look at its treatment of juvenile offenders and how its treatment may be contributing to their future delinquency. More specifically, the juvenile justice system must be scrutinized and urged to utilize empirically based models of treatment as an alternative to incarceration. Although advocacy and policy are great avenues for change in the treatment of delinquents, real changes take place in the relationship between delinquents and their service delivery professionals (i.e., case managers, clinicians, paraprofessionals). Therefore it is important that service delivery professionals receive adequate training and educational opportunities to become more knowledgeable about delinquency. The lack of training can lead to ineffective treatment approaches and the potential for further harm.

It is imperative that delinquency research continues. Future research should continue to look at variables that may contribute to the rise in delinquency. However, further exploration of delinquency and variables specific to their rise in recidivism, may assist in programming and effective treatment modalities that target their needs. Further research should include not only variables that may be impacting delinquency, but also those variables that may be preventing an adolescent from becoming delinquent. This will offer the opportunity for future prevention and earlier intervention. Future research should be conducted on qualitative interviews with clients, parents, and treatment providers, exploring treatment motivation among juvenile offenders and continued evaluation of treatments effectiveness.

REFERENCES

Calhoun, G., Jurgens, J., & Chen, F. (1993). The neophyte female delinquent: A review of the literature. *Adolescence, 28*(110), 460.

Cunningham, P.B. & Hennggeler, S.W. (2001). Implementation of an empirically based drug and violence prevention and intervention program in public school settings. *Journal of Clinical Child Psychology, 30*, 221-233. Retrieved November 16, 2004, from Academic Search Premier database.

Haghighi, B. & Lopez, A. (1993). Success/failure of group home treatment programs for juveniles. *Federal Probation, 57*, 53-59. Retrieved November 16, 2004 from Academic Search Premier database.

Juvenile Delinquency Prevention Program Fact Sheet. (2004). New York State Juvenile Delinquency Prevention Program. Retrieved November 2, 2004, from http://criminaljustice.state.ny.us/ofpa/juvdelprevfactsheet.htm

Kadish, T.E., Glaser, B.A., Calhoun, G.B., & Risler, E.A. (1999). Counseling juvenile Offenders: A program evaluation. *Journal of Addictions & Offender Counseling, 19*, 88-95. Retrieved November 16, 2004 from Academic Search Premier database.

Kurtz, A. (2002). What works for delinquency? The effectiveness of interventions for teenage offending behaviour. *The Journal of Forensic Psychiatry, 13*, 671-688.

Lipsey, M.W. & Wilson, D.B. (1998). *Effective intervention for serious juvenile offenders: A synthesis of research.* In R. Loeber & D.P. Farrington (Eds.), Serious & violent juvenile offenders: Risk factors and successful interventions (p. 313-345). Thousand Oaks, CA: Sage.

Miller, K.E. (2003). Effectiveness of school-based violence prevention programs. *American Family Physician, 67*, 161-166. Retrieved November 16, 2004 from Academic Search Premier database.

Roy, S. (1995). Juvenile restitution and recidivism in a midwestern county. *Federal Probation, 59*, 55-63. Retrieved November 16, 2004 from Academic Search Premier database.

Quinn, W.H. & Van Dyke, D.J. (2004). A multiple family group intervention for first-Time offenders: Comparisons with probation and dropouts on recidivism. *Journal of Community Psychology, 32*, 177-200.

Thornberry, T.P., Huizinga, D., & Loeber, R. (2004). The causes and correlates studies: Findings and policy implications. *Juvenile Justice*, IX, 3-17. Varied Violence Prevention Programs Prove Effective. (2002) *Inside School Safety, 7*, 4-5.

doi:10.1300/J394v04n01_06

Medication Adherence Among Older Adults

Julie H. Grocki, CMSW
Katie Kattic Huffman, BSSW

SUMMARY. With the dramatic demographic changes that are resulting in the "graying of America" has come a substantial interest in the health and health concerns of older adults. The increasing incidence and prevalence of systemic diseases, especially chronic diseases among elders, and the concomitant increase in medication use, have provided impetus for the study of medication adherence among older adults. This study examined barriers to effective medication adherence among 67 persons 60 years of age and older from closed case files of an Adult Protective Services (APS) agency. A Crosstabulation analysis was conducted to examine gender differences. Results revealed that for both males and females, intentional caregiver neglect (41% and 36% respectively) was the predominant barrier while dementia was the second (24% males and 41% females). A One-Way ANOVA was conducted to compare means and revealed that for the entire sample, intentional caregiver neglect was the predominant barrier to effective medication adherence (37%) while drug abuse (3%) was the least likely. Findings indicate that a significant number of the elderly do not adhere to medication protocols. As a result, risk

Julie H. Grocki (E-mail: Jgrocki@utk.edu) and Katie Kattic Huffman (E-mail: khuffan@utk.edu) are affiliated with The University of Tennessee, College of Social Work, Knoxville, TN 37996.

[Haworth co-indexing entry note]: "Medication Adherence Among Older Adults." Grocki, Julie H., and Katie Kattic Huffman. Co-published simultaneously in *Journal of Evidence-Based Social Work* (The Haworth Press, Inc.) Vol. 4, No. 1/2, 2007, pp. 97-120; and: *Building Excellence: The Rewards and Challenges of Integrating Research into the Undergraduate Curriculum* (ed: Catherine N. Dulmus, and Karen M. Sowers) The Haworth Press, 2007, pp. 97-120. Single or multiple copies of this article are available for a fee from The Haworth Document Delivery Service [1-800-HAWORTH, 9:00 a.m. - 5:00 p.m. (EST). E-mail address: docdelivery@haworthpress.com].

for serious health consequences of medication non-adherence is likely. The need for further research is discussed given these findings. doi: 10.1300/J394v04n01_07 *[Article copies available for a fee from The Haworth Document Delivery Service: 1-800-HAWORTH. E-mail address: <docdelivery@haworthpress.com> Website: <http://www.HaworthPress.com> © 2007 by The Haworth Press, Inc. All rights reserved.]*

KEYWORDS. Medication, older, adults

INTRODUCTION

Currently in the United States, there are 38 million citizens over the age of 65. This accounts for approximately 13% of the total U.S. population. It is expected that this will increase to 20% of the population by 2030 (Administration on Aging [AoA], 2005, statistics). This historically unprecedented population increase among the elderly (often referred to as "the graying of America") has resulted in increased research associated with the health and well-being of the elderly. Specific attention has been given recently to the issue of medication adherence among the elderly (Edwards, 1995). Medication adherence is particularly important for the elderly because of age-associated onset of chronic diseases. Drug therapy can offer symptomatic relief for the elderly and can assist in preventing the onset of disabling and life-threatening complications. Prevention is correlated with medication utilization/adherence among older adults (Stockton and Jones, 1993).

Many studies have shown that in the US and Canada, prescription drug utilization increases significantly with age (Centers for Disease Control and Prevention [CDC], 2005, NHANES; Kaufman, Kelley & Rosenberg 2002; Quinn, Baker & Evans, 1989) especially among women (Ganguli, 1996; Gilbert, Luszcz & Owen, 1993; Rosenberg & Moore, 1997). Studies have estimated that in persons aged 60 and older, nonadherence to medication regimens varies from 40% to 75% (Hughes, 2004) to approximately 50% with a range from 26-59% in those 60 years and older (van Eijken, Tsang, Wensing, & Grol, 2003). Some estimates report that one half of patients in clinical care take their medications incorrectly (Urqhuart, 1994). The results of Peterson, Takiya, and Finley (2003) suggests that medication nonadherence accounts for approximately 10% of all hospital admissions and 23% of nursing home admissions in the United States. The proportion of hospitalizations among older patients attributable to nonadherence has been reported to be as high as 11% (Col, Fanale, & Kronholm, 1990; Grymonpre, Mitenko, & Sitar, 1988; McKenney & Harrison, 1976; Vik, Maxwell, & Hogan, 2004).

While age is generally not considered to be predictive of medication nonadherence, among older persons this issue has particular relevance because of the disproportionate amount of drugs consumed by this population. For older adults, the problem of medication nonadherence increases as the number of medical conditions equiring the utilization of medications increases (Weintraub, 1990). The disproportionate use of medications combined with age-related pharmacokinetic and pharmacodynamic changes, places older adults at increased risk for medication related problems (MRPs).

The use of at least three or more drugs is common among older adults. It is estimated that as high as 25% of the total U.S. population are prescribed three or more drugs. These data suggest that this places elderly people at particular risk for poor medication adherence. Problems also arise when dementia or depression are present which may interfere with memory and thus effect medication adherence Salzman, 1995). Averages of drug utilization among elderly hospitalized patients suggest that eight drugs taken simultaneously may be typical (Salzman, 1995). These staggering statistics lead to increased medication nonadherence and significant clinical and economic consequences.

High rates of medication utilization by older people raise a number of issues ranging from concerns with rising expenditures for individuals and third-party insurers, increased risk of adverse drug reactions, and toxic or interactional effects from concomitant use of multiple pharmaceutical and over the counter (OTC) agents. Ingestion of a greater number of different medications clearly exposes individuals to a higher risk of adverse reactions and interactions (Stockton & Jones, 1993).

Medications can serve and be of great benefit to the elderly however, misapplication and misuse of medications may result in undesirable outcomes. Many factors are associated with medication nonadherence and related health outcomes in older adults. Some of these factors associated with aging are the commonality of marginal health literacy, physical disability, a lack of social and family support, poor financial resources and caregiver variables such as dependence. These all complicate the ability of older adults to adhere to prescription and nonprescription medication regimens (Murray et al., 2004). Other factors related to poor medication adherence among older adults are decrease in or loss of visual and/or auditory acuity, cognitive impairment, unpleasant side effects and comorbid conditions (McGraw and Drennan, 2001; Urquhart & Chevalley, 1988).

What is unique about older adults is their greater sensitivity to medications, greater propensity for the development of adverse effects, and greater complexity of medication regimens as chronic illnesses develop throughout the course of their lives. These unique physical conditions and specific barriers that impact effective medication utilization cause older adults to be more vulnerable to incorrect utilization of medications. Older adults respond less predictably than younger adults to most medications, typically requiring lower daily doses to achieve the desired therapeutic effect and minimize adverse effects and toxicity. This unpredictability is particularly evident among the frail elderly, that is, those at the age of 80 and older (AoA, 2005, statistics) who often suffer from central neurodegenerative disorders and/or significant burdens of comorbid medical problems (Kuzuya et al., 2000).

The most common medication nonadherent behavior reported of the elderly appears to be underuse of a prescribed drug. Inappropriate drug discontinuation may occur in up to 40% of prescribing situations, particularly within the first year of a chronic care regimen. As many as 10% of elderly people may take drugs prescribed for others and more than 20% may take drugs not currently prescribed by a physician. This phenomenon is not new and is an old central problem of cooperation between physician and patient (Salzman, 1995).

It is estimated that 40-45% of elderly individuals are unable to take their medications as prescribed (Morrow, Leirer, & Sheikh, 1988). Low medication adherence is increasingly recognized as a dominant feature in elderly patients (Gray, Mahoney, & Blough, 2001). This may be the result of forgetfulness, avoidance of troublesome adverse effects, cognitive decline, physical inability to self-administer medications, economic limitations and intentional under-dosage (MacLaughlin, Raehl, Treadway et al., 2005). Medication nonadherence is a major issue in the healthcare of older persons which can lead to therapeutic failure and poor utilization of resources (Edwards,1995; Klein, Turvey, & Wallace, 2004; Weintraub, 1990). It is clear that medication nonadherence to both prescribed and non prescribed medication regimens has a significant negative clinical impact on the older person, their loved ones and the medical establishment especially in regards to fiscal expenditures.

LITERATURE REVIEW

The literature on medication adherence has grown substantially over the past 4 decades (Vik et al., 2004). Most studies have highlighted the negative impacts of nonadherence on patient well-being and healthcare costs. This literature review was conducted using the search terms: Medication compliance/noncompliance, elderly, older, adult, medication adherence/nonadherence and prescription drugs. Databases searched were: CINAHL, Medline, EBSCO, Psyche Info and Social Work Abstracts. Hard copies and on-line journals were retrieved along with national Websites. All studies noted have been conducted on persons 60 and older. This literature review is organized into the following sections: Definitions, reasons for medication nonadherence, age variables, predictors of medication nonadherence, literacy, medical variables, medication-related variables, behavior and belief variables, what impacts medication nonadherence, consequences of medication nonadherence and assessment of medication nonadherence.

Definitions

The literature defines medication adherence as "the extent to which a person's behavior (in terms of taking medication, following diets, or executing lifestyle changes) coincides with medical or health advice" (Vik et al., 2004, p. 304). Medication adherence may also be defined as "the extent to which a person's or caregiver medication administration behavior coincides with medical advice (MacLaughlin et al., 2005, p. 232). Medication nonadherence is the opposite of this. Ideally a collaborative relationship between the patient (or caregiver and his/her healthcare provider) is required for successful medication adherence and the term should include diet, exercise and lifestyle activities (MacLaughlin et al., 2005).

The older term used for medication adherence was "medication compliance" A one-way relationship is implied with the term "compliance" whereby the healthcare provider gives instructions with minimal or no input from the patients. This term has underlying paternalistic and omnipotent overtones. It also places full responsibility of proper medication-taking behavior on the patient. A patient under this term is labeled derogatorily because he/she does not comply with a prescribed regimen regardless of how complicated, unreasonable or expensive the medication taking may be (Edwards, 1993; MacLaughlin et al., 2005; Salzman, 1995, Weintraub, 1990). With this term, it seems that the healthcare provider is inconsiderate of the lifestyle, health habits and the economic means of the patients.

The studies conducted on medication adherence have generally been limited to the administration of oral prescription drugs. All of the empirical studies found in this literature review relate specifically to the administration of prescribed drugs save for one. The single study found measuring over the counter [OTC] medications and herbal products among older persons indicated that among community-dwelling well-educated seniors, a mean number of different 5.9 prescriptions medications, 3.5 OTC and .4 herbal were taken daily (Raehl, Bond, & Woods, 2002). The self-administration of OTC and herbal products are often overlooked when assessing for medication adherence. The efficacy of medication regimens may be substantially influenced by these factors (Haynes, McDonald, Garg et al., 2002; Vik et al., 2005). Physicians are usually not aware of self-medication regimens unless the patient or caregiver volunteers this information. The methods to assess medication adherence are subjective and remain potentially biased.

Reasons for Medication Medication Nonadherence

Various underlying reasons may affect medication adherence. Balkrishnan, (1998) developed a classification scheme that assigned these reasons into categories: demographic, medical, medication, behavioral, and economic. Each of the 5 areas may be noted as being a potential positive or negative factor impacting the patient's ability to adhere to prescribed medication regimens. Frequently, a combination of these categories leads to medication nonadherence (Balkrishnan, 1998). Identification of patient-specific variables that influence medication adherence can be included in a comprehensive medical history and recorded in a patient's medical record in the same way that the family and social history are noted.

Age Variables

It is often assumed that increasing age is associated with medication adherence (Coons, Sheahan, & Martin, 1994; Cooper, Love, & Raffoul, 1982). Medication-taking behavior varies across the aging continuum. Park, Morrell, and Frieske et al. (1992) observed of adults 71 year of age and older demonstrated more nonadherence than the young-old adults (70 and less than years of age). The cause of underadherence by the group 71 years and older was found to result from omissions of medications.

High medication adherence rates (greater than 80%) were found in a study of older adults between 65 and 74 years of age as assessed by prescription claims data among Medicaid enrollees (Monane, Bohn, & Gurwitz et al., 1996).

Predictors of Medication Nonadherence

There have been a number of studies that have identified potential predictors of medication adherence or nonadherence in chronic disease states common in the elderly such as chronic obstructive pulmonary disease, breast cancer and cardiovascular disease (hypertension, congestive heart failure and glaucoma (MacLaughlin et al., 2005). Cognition is also a large determinant of medication nonadherence. Cognitive impairment (MMSE scores 24 or less) has been reported (Gray, Mahoney, & Blugh, 2001) to be associated with both over and under-adherence of medications. Isaac and Tamblyn (1993) determined that visual memory skills also appear to correlate with medication adherence. Depression has been found to be associated with under adherence (Ciechanowski, Katon, & Russo, 2000; Wang, Bohn, & Knight, 2002) and depression screening is warranted when medication nonadherence is suspected.

Literacy

Inadequate or marginal functional health literacy is a contributing factor to high incidences of medication nonadherence in the elderly. The definition of functional health literacy includes the ability to read and understand patient-specific medication instructions, read prescription labels and the manufacturer's package insert and act on this health information (Andrus & Roth, 2002). Health literacy is not correlated strongly with years of schooling or education level. In older persons, functional health literacy is markedly lower even after adjusting for gender, race, ethnicity, cognition, visual acuity and years of education (Baker, Gazmararian, & Sudano, 2000). Inadequate or marginal health literacy was found in up to 35% of English speaking US Medicare–managed care enrollees in (Scott, Gazmararian, & Williams, 2002). Literacy skills of older patients are rarely assessed by healthcare practitioners even though screening tools are available (Health literacy, 1999). One screening instrument for health literacy is the Short Test of Functional Health Literacy in Adults Test. This takes 7 minutes to complete and maybe administered by medical office staff or nursing assistants (Baker, Williams, & Parker, 1999). Other measures of functional health literacy are having patients read a short passage of a book to proper medical staff. Illiterate patients will often avoid this embarrassment by making an excuse not to read.

Medical Variables

Older adults are at a particularly high risk of medication nonadherence from medical related variables such as disease, severity and direction of illness, number of co morbid conditions, frequency of use of medical services, satisfaction with healthcare providers and quality of care (Balkrishnan, 1998). Older adults often have decreased visual and auditory acuity and manual dexterity which frequently leads to difficulty in reading prescription labels, differentiating pill colors and opening prescription vials (Ruscin & Semla, 1996). Cognitive impairment, increased psychological stress as a result of lack of social support, dependence upon caregivers, frustration with physical disabilities and depression are other predictors of poor adherence (Coons et al., 1994; DiMatteo, Lepper, & Croghan, 2000; Ruscin and Semla, 1996). Frequently due to cognitive impairment, the elderly often do not recall their own medical conditions which can be quite numerous. Raehl et al. (2002) reported a mean of 6.11 specific medical conditions per subject in their study of community-dwelling seniors. Out of these, only half of the conditions were spontaneously recalled by the older adult studied. The other half of medical conditions were identified by the interviewer prompting recall.

Medication Related Variables

Poor medication adherence has been presumed to be associated with the administration regimen of numerous medications (Stewart, 1991) that may be a risk factor for nonadherence leading to hospitalization (Col, Fanale, & Kronholm, 1990). Administration regimen, type of medication, drug delivery system, therapeutic regimen and adverse effects are medication–related variables that may influence adherence (Balkrishnan, 1998; Peterson, Takiya, & Finley, 2003). No significant differences have been found between adherence rates that have a once or twice daily regimen. Multiple studies on patients with a broad range of ages and disease states have consistently found that medications with a twice daily or more frequency are associated with decreased adherence (Christensen, Williams, & Goldberg, 1997; Claxton, Cramer, & Pierce, 2001; Cramer, Mattson, & Prevey, 1989; Cramer, Vachon, &

Desforges, 1995; Eisen, Miller, & Woodward et al., 1990; Kruse, Eggert-Kruse, & Rampmaier, 1991; Pullar, Birtwell, & Wiles, 1988; Taggart, Johnston, & McDevitt, 1981; Tinkelman, Vanderpool, & Carroll, 1980).

A high number of chronic conditions and use of a large number of concurrent drugs is positively associated with poor adherence (Billups, Malone, & Carter, 2000). Sharkness and Snow (1992) found that the use of one or more drugs was associated with worse adherence. The relationship between the number of medications taken on a daily basis may appear more complicated than appears between the number of medications and adherence.

A review of 26 medication adherence studies resulted in findings of a 70% adherence rate of once daily administration regimens versus 70% with twice daily regimens. Yet, as the frequency of administration increased to more than a twice daily regimen, drastic decreases in adherence were noted (52%) with three times daily administration regimens and 42% with four times daily administration (Greenberg, 1984). The small differences found in this study suggests that adherence between once or twice daily administration regimens signifies that little benefit or possible harm may occur with switching from a twice daily to a once daily regimen. An older individual may be placed more at risk if he/she forgets to take a single dose of a drug that is given only once daily. This may place the patient more at risk than forgetting to take a single dose of a twice daily prescribed medication. Certain medications are termed "forgiving drugs" in that they have a blunted response when one or two doses are missed (Boissel & Nony, 2002). A "forgiving drug" reduces the clinical consequences of a missed dose as greater variability in timing of doses is permitted. Many pharmaceutical manufacturers today are reformulating products to provide for extended administration frequencies such as once weekly administrations.

An evaluation of adherence with once weekly transdermal clonidine versus once daily sustained released oral clonidine (Burris, Papademetrious, & Wallin, 1991) found increased adherence with the once weekly administration. Adherence rates in another 12 week study (de Klerk, 2001) of once weekly administration regimens of fluoxetine versus once daily administration regimens found during the first month similar adherence rates, yet past month 1, adherence rates declined with those taking once daily fluoxetine. Medication adherence may also be impacted by concurrent medications being taken by an individual. The elderly frequently require multiple medications for multiple chronic diseases (MacLaughlin et al., 2005; Raehl et al., 2002). Intentional non-adherence to prescription drug regimens may be caused by disappointment with traditional prescribed medicines and enthusiasm for alternative medicines.

Behavior and Belief Variables

Patient's knowledge and various sociobehavioral characteristics such as the patient's knowledge, understanding and beliefs about their diseases and medications have been found to significantly impact medication adherence (Balkrishnan, 1998; Lakshman, Fernando, & Kazarian, 1995; Lin, Spiga, & Fortsch, 1979; Sharkness & Snow, 1992; Stewart, 1989). Better adherence is found among those who understand their disease and perceived need for treatment (Col, Fanale, & Kronholm, 1990; Lakshman et al., 1995; Sharkness & Snow, 1992). This leads many to the conclusion that knowledge about diseases and their consequences is a positive factor influencing adherence. One controlled study however clearly indicated that improved medication adherence is not alone impacted by increased knowledge of the disease state (Peterson, Takiya, & Finley, 2003).

Several behavioral patterns of medication nonadherence have been observed. A commonly observed behavior is improvement in medication adherence several days prior to a scheduled medical examination. This is often termed: "White Coat Compliance" or "The Tooth Brush Effect" (Pullar 1991, p . 51) and this may substantially overestimate patient adherence. The patient often portrays good adherence to please the healthcare provider or to be perceived as a good patient. This has been found to be particularly true for medications in which drug serum concentrations must be drawn at scheduled clinic visits (Cramer, Scheyer, & Mattson, 1990; Feinstein, 1990).

It is frequently presumed that poor unintentional medication adherence is a result of forgetfulness, yet this is not always the case. Cooper et al. (1982) found unintentional nonadherence to account for less than 30% of participants in their study while 71% were intentionally not adhering to their medication regimen. The reasons noted for intentional medication nonadherence were the perceptions that the medication was not needed (52%), there were adverse effects occurring (15%), or the patient needed more of the prescribed drug than was prescribed (4%).

Utilizing behavioral medicine principles, Garfield and Caro (2000) have proposed that adherence may be improved and substantiated by assessment and movement through the following stages of change: (1) Preconception; the patient is not intending to change, (2) Contemplation; the patient considers change, (3) Preparation; small changes are initiated,

(4) Action; active behavioral changes are made; and (5) Maintenance; there is sustained long-term change in the behavior. Recognition of which stage the patient may be in enables the physician to recommended an appropriate intervention aimed at increasing adherence (Willey, Redding, & Stafford et al., 2000).

What Impacts Medication Nonadherence

Adherence may be profoundly impacted by disease characteristics such as cognitive and functional decline. Diminished functional abilities are those that are visual, auditory, olfactory and sensate. Older patients may have difficulty distinguishing between pill colors, particularly blue-green and yellow as well as the size or measurement of liquid elixirs (Hurd & Blevins, 1984; Hurd & Butkovich, 1986). They often have difficulty opening child-proof medication lids or smaller medication containers (Hurd & Butkovich, 1986; Keram & Williams, 1988). The inability to read prescription labels and to open prescription vials is found to be associated with medication nonadherence (Murray, Darnell, & Weinberger et al., 1986). More medication errors are also associated with mixed labeling (Morrell, Park, & Poon, 1990).

Older persons may take what is known as a "drug holiday" of less forgiving drugs such as the cardiovascular agents, because of a lack of financial resources. This patient-initiated discontinuation of drugs is clearly associated with increased physician visits and hospitalizations (Meredith, 1996). Col et al., 1990) found that economic factors and adverse effects were the most common reasons for nonadherence.

Consequences of Medication Nonadherence

Very few patients of any age are able to adhere perfectly to a prescribed medication regimen (Urquhart, 1994). In the elderly, the consequences of medication non adherence are profound often leading to significant morbidity and mortality.

Weintraub (1990) noted from nonadherence among the elderly, a lack of maximum efficacy, annoying nuisance side effects, diminishing quality-of-life, and life-threatening adverse outcomes. This also has a negative economic impact in healthcare systems (Shelton, Fritsch, & Scott, 2000).

Col et al. (1990) found in their study of patients of hospitals admissions, 28% to be medication related with nonadherence accounting for 11% of that group and 17% because of adverse drug reactions. A more recent study of elderly patients aged 75 and older (Chan, Nicklason, & Vial, 2001) found 26% of hospital admissions collectively were a result of medication nonadherence, omission and cessation of medication regimen. Direct costs of medication nonadherence in the elderly are hospitalizations, re-hospitalizations and nursing home admissions. Medication nonadherence may also result in disease progression, leading to a much greater human and economic toll (MacLaughlin et al., 2005).

Assessment of Medication Adherence

While assessment of medication adherence is essential in the elderly, no single traditional method of assessing medication adherence has been found to be reliable even when used by pharmacists (Haynes, McDonald, & Garg, 2002; Roter, Hall, & Merisca, 1998; Secnik, Pathak, & Cohen, (2000). Pharmacists may use prescription refill records along with pill counts which are often unreliable as a screening tool for nonadherence as they cannot prove that a person is actually taking the medication (Haynes et al., 2002; Pullar, Kumar, & Tindall, 1989). Clinicians often rely upon patient and caregiver self-reports which are also unreliable.

Economic factors and a subsequent ability to pay assessment play an increasing role in medication adherence assessments especially in countries that have a capitalist healthcare system. In such countries, the patient's socioeconomic status, type of insurance coverage and costs of medications and general medical care may combine with rising medication copayments to render prescription drugs unaffordable.

Nevertheless, all of the assessment methods noted to measure medication adherence have poor reliability and may either overestimate or underestimate medication adherence behavior (Cramer, 1995). Medication management tools are subjected to observer bias and may not reflect a patient's private behavior (Edelberg, Shallenberger, and Wei, 2000; Fitten, Coleman, & Siembieda, 1995; Meyer and Schuna, 1989; Raehl, Bond, & Woods, 2002). Hence, a combination of assessment methods may be preferred.

One study (Pullar, Kumar, & Tindall, 1989) measured adherence by returned pill containers and found these to grossly overestimate adherence and a poor pharmacological indicator. Return pill containers and prescription refill data were also found to overestimate medication adherence (Paes, Bakker, & Soe-Agnie, 1998). Another study's results (Rudd, Byyny, & Zachary, 1989) reported weekly pill counts masking excessive medication taking. Pill dumping is a known pattern that patients engage in when they are aware that the prescriber may suspect non-adherence. At present there is generally no accepted reliable measurement instrument for medication adherence for the elderly or those of other age groups. The majority of medication adherence studies have employed indirect measures. The most practical method of medication adherence assessment is for most elderly patients to have a patient or caregiver interact with the medication prescriber using open-ended non-threatening and nonjudgmental questions. The information obtained from all of these assessment methods are largely inadequate (Haynes, McDonald, & Garg, 2002). The most accurate assessment of medication nonadherence is if the elder experiences a decline in functional or cognitive abilities (Chan, Nicklason, & Vial, 2001; Vik et al., 2004).

METHODS

Data Collection

One hundred sixty two closed case files of community-dwelling and residential older persons 60 and older from an Adult Protective Services (APS) agency were examined. The case files were open from the period of January 2001 to September, 2003. Data was collected between October 2003 to February 2004. Case file inclusion criteria for the study was the following: (1) Clients had been over the age of 60 and (2) client assessment noted them as "nonadherent with medication(s)" anywhere on the assessment intake form. A total of 26% of the files met the inclusion criteria (N = 67). All case files were referrals to Adult Protective Services to be assessed for substantiated cases of elder abuse and neglect or self-neglect. The case worker had determined if medication nonadherence had occurred and the reasons for medication nonadherence. Specific factors noted to impact alleged medication nonadherence were: Intentional caregiver neglect, dementia of the older person, drug abuse by the caregiver, mental illness of the older person, theft by the caregiver, and a lack of family or social support for the older person. The intake assessments contained structured and semi structured questionnaires completed by a trained interviewer. Barriers to proper medication adherence were noted on the intake form. This study was approved by an accredited state university in the United States Human Subject Review Committee and the Department of Human Services: Adult Protective

Services. Post data collection, barriers to effective medication adherence were examined.

STATISTICAL EVALUATION OF DATA

All results were initially described and plotted to enhance familiarisation with the data. All of the variables drawn from the collected data were evaluated for their impact on medication adherence. Nonadherence was the dependent variable while the independent variables were: Age, gender, intentional caregiver neglect, dementia, drug abuse of the caregiver, theft by the caregiver, mental illness of the older person, and a lack of social and family support for the older person. A Crosstabulation analysis was conducted to identify evidence of predictors of nonadherence for dependence on gender and reason and a Oneway ANOVA was conducted to compare the means of the groups.

RESULTS

Information on the closed cases confirmed that all participants in the study group were age 60 and over (mean age: 77, range: 60-97). The gender distribution of the population group was 50 females (75%) and 17 males (26%). The mean age of the entire sample was 77, with females mean age 77, (range 60-97) and males, mean age of 76 (range: 63-94). A number of variables considered as individual barriers associated with medication adherence were analyzed using Crosstabulation analysis. These data are summarized in Table 1. Crosstabulation analysis results indicate that for females, intentional caregiver neglect (36%) was the predominant barrier to effective medication adherence while drug abuse (2%) of the caregiver was the least. For males, intentional caregiver neglect (41%) was also the predominant barrier to medication adherence while theft by the caregiver (0%) was the least likely. Dementia interestingly was the second common barrier to effective medication adherence for females (41%) and for males (24%), although this equaled the significance of support system for males. Results indicated no statistical significance for gender on barriers to medication adherence.

A One-Way ANOVA was conducted to compare means (see Table 2). The Levene test proved to be nonsignificant. Interestingly, the findings of the One-Way ANOVA indicated that for whole sample (N = 67), intentional caregiver neglect was the predominant barrier to effective

TABLE 1. Crosstabs

Gender*Reason Crosstabulation
Count

		Reason						Total
		Caregiver	Dementia	Drug Abuse	Mental Health	Theft	Support	
Gender	F	18	12	1	9	4	6	50
	M	7	4	1	1	0	4	17 .
Total		25	16	2	10	4	10	67

Chi-Square Tests

	Value	Df	Asymp.Sig. (2 sided)
Pearson Chi-Square	4.471	5	.484
Likelihood Ratio	5.520	5	.356
N of Valid Cases	67		

TABLE 2. Oneway

Descriptives

	N	Mean	Std. Deviation	Std. Error	95% Confidence Interval for Mean	
					Lower Bound	Upper Bound
Caregiver	25	77.760	10.3170	2.0634	73.501	82.019
Dementia	16	80.688	9.3075	2.3269	75.728	85.647
Drug	2	66.000	.0000	.0000	66.000	66.000
Mental	10	72.700	9.7417	3.0806	65.731	79.669
Theft	4	73.500	5.8023	2.9011	64.267	82.733
Support	10	75.800	8.2704	2.6153	69.884	81.716
Total	67	76.806	9.6487	1.1788	74.452	79.159

Levine's Test of Homogeneity of Variance

Age

Levene Statistic	df1	df2	Sig.
1.693	5	61	.150

medication adherence (37%) while drug abuse (3%) was the least likely. In order of significance, the issues most likely to cause medication nonadherence were: Intentional caregiver neglect (37%), dementia, (24%), mental illness and family and social support (15%), theft (6%) and drug abuse (3%). For the oldest men age, 81, dementia was the predominant barrier. Drug abuse was the predominant barrier youngest men (age 66).

While the Crosstabulation and One-Way ANOVA yielded much useful information regarding relationships between individual variables and medication adherence, statistical significance was not achieved when measuring the impact of gender on barriers to medication adherence. As well, none of the tests provided insights into how variables might jointly affect adherence behavior. This is important to examine as most older persons have multiple health problems.

The information related to nonadherence in these data is limited as it does not differentiate between the person who may experience medication adherence due to intentional or unintentional self-neglect. The predominant variables analyzed related to the caregiver, except for dementia and mental illness. Results from this study are limited due to the case selection criteria. Since cases were restricted to those elderly reported for abuse or neglect the findings from this study should be used with caution. This study does indicate some important findings relevant to medication adherence for older adults who have been abuse or neglected, either intentionally or unintentionally. For instance, it does appear that this population does indeed have difficulty with medication adherence. This medical problem is by no means limited to physician's records, long-term care facilities or hospital admissions records. It is well recognized that reported nonadherence is probably a gross underestimate of actual non-adherence (MacLaughlin et al., 2005). It appears that a rather simple questionnaire can detect medication nonadherence and may be useful in a variety of medical practice settings. The questions in the APS assessment may not be sufficiently sensitive in usefully predicting persons who may be poor adherers, but they do identify important independent risk factors which could be considered in clinical practice. The most strongly associated risk factor for both groups was intentional caregiver neglect. This makes sense given that the cases were substantiated to be opened by the Adult Protective Services agency to investigate abuse and neglect allegations.

This present research indicates that the variables studied may be significant factors impacting medication nonadherence among older persons who do not have reports filed with APS. These factors should be examined more closely in assessments given by a patient's primary care physician and hospital admission intakes. Future research may be able to determine if these factors are significant. Individual associations with self reported nonadherence have been noted and clearly identified, but an accurate predictive model for adherence behavior in unintentional cases for the elderly remains elusive. As noted, the assessment tools for medication adherence or nonadherence are limited and fallible. However, all medication adherence studies use one or more of the assessment tools noted in this document.

DISCUSSION

This study provides important information about medication adherence among older adults 60 and over who have substantiated reports of elder abuse and neglect in an Adult Protective Services agency. To the author's knowledge this is a first study of its kind. The results found indications that medication nonadherence is substantial (26%) in reports of elder abuse and neglect. It must be noted that only 16% of elder abuse and neglect situations are referred for help while 84% remain unreported (National Center on Elder Abuse, 2005, abuse statistics). From this, we can infer that the findings of this study may only be the tip of the iceberg. Further research is warranted in the area of medication nonadherence with APS cases on a wider basis.

There is a large gap in the literature on medication adherence that differentiates between OTC, prescription medications and alternative medicine products such as herbal remedies and other forms of medicine (i.e., acupuncture). There are also gaps on the impact that caregivers alone have upon medication adherence among community-dwelling older persons that are not being abused/neglected. There is a large gap on income or "ability to pay" assessment studies. Gaps have been found as well on evaluating the appropriateness of the drug regimens older persons are given and the impact adherence and nonadherence may have on relevant health outcomes.

There is a large amount of literature focusing on factors that impact medication adherence but few studies on the actual relevance of medication nonadherence. This may be attributed to the poor accuracy of the current medication adherence tools. While there is some evidence that medication nonadherence may have a detrimental impact on health outcomes, there is a gap in the literature on how nonadherence may actually be beneficial. Gaps have also been found on measuring the appropriateness of the drug regimens that patients are on as older persons may self-modify their medication regimens to mitigate adverse negative side effects (Vik et al., 2004).

Healthcare professionals should devote more time to ensuring their older patients understand newly prescribed medication regimens, their side effects and the impact that proper adherence may have (Morrell, Parj, & Poon, 1989). Programs which help secure resources such as providing economic relief for medications may significantly improve adherence and clinical outcomes (MacLaughlin et al., 2005; Paris, Dunham, & Sebastian, 1999; Schoen, DiDomenico, & Connor, 2001). The literature indicates that routine assessment of medication adherence in the elderly is rarely performed in everyday clinical practice (Vik et al., 2004). This may reflect the inherent difficulty of accurately assessing and measuring medication administration and the general ineffectiveness of programs designed to improve medication adherence. Medication adherence is critical for the older person to achieve and maintain optimal physical and mental health outcomes.

Strategies such as careful labeling, self-administration of medicine programmers, simplifying drug regimens and the use of medication adherence devices can help to promote patient adherence. Some of these interventions will assist for certain older persons, however a multidisciplinary assessment and a regular review of each person's ability to adhere to medication should be undertaken. It is important to monitor medication adherence and how these changes affect the elders identified at risk especially with the new Medicare prescription dug plans being implemented (Klein, Turvey, & Wallanc 2004).

The issue of medication adherence among persons 60 and older has been substantiated. The consequences of medication nonadherence may be serious in older persons. It is hoped that assertive measures will be developed and implemented to ameliorate the commonality of this medical issue among older persons in the United States.

REFERENCES

Administration on Aging [AoA] (2004). *Statistics: Aging the 21st century.* Retrieved August 1st, 2005 from: http://aoa.gov/prof/Statistics/future_growth/aging21/preface.asp

Andrus, M., & Roth, M. (2002). Health literacy: A review. *Pharmacotherapy, 22*(3), 282-302.

Baker, D., Gazmararian, J., Sudano, J., & Patterson, M. (2000). The association between age and health literacy among elderly persons. *Journal of Gerontology B
Psychological Sciences, 55B*(6), S368-S374.

Baker, D., Williams, M., Parker, R., Gazmararian, J., & Nurss, J. (1999). Development
of a brief test to measure functional health literacy. *Patient Education Council,
38*(1), 33-42.

Balkrishnan, R. (1998). Predictors of medication adherence in the elderly. *Clinical
Therapist, 20*(3), 764-771.

Billups, S., Malone, D., & Carter, B. (2000). The relationship between drug therapy
noncompliance and patients characteristics, health-related quality of life, and health
care costs. *Pharamacotherapy, 20*(8), 941-949.

Boissel, J., & Nony, P. (2002) Using pharmacokinetic-pharmacodynamic relationships
to predict the effect of poor compliance. *Clinical Pharmacokinetics, 41*(1), 1-6.

Burris, J., Papademetrious, V., & Wallin, J. (1991). Therapeutic adherence in the elderly: Transdermal clonidine compared to oral verapamil for hypertension. *American Journal of Medicine, 91*(1), 22S-28S.

Cartwright, A. (1990). Medicine taking by people aged 65 or more. *British Medical
Bulletin, 46*(1), 63-76.

Centers for Disease Control and Prevention [CDC].(2005). NHANES Data Brief.
Retrieved August 20, 2005 from: http://www.cdc.gov/nchs/about/major/nhanes/
Databriefs.htm

Chan, M., Nicklason, F., & Vial, J. (2001). Adverse drug events as a cause of hospital
admissions in the elderly. *Internal Medicine Journal, 31*(1), 199-205.

Christensen, D., Williams, B., & Goldberg, D. (1997). Assessing compliance to antihypertensive medications using computer-based pharmacy records. *Medical Care,
35*(8), 1164-1170.

Ciechanowski, P., Katon, W., & Russo, J. (2000). Depression and diabetes: Impact of
depressive symptoms on adherence, function, and costs. *Archives of Internal Medicine, 160*(21), 3278-3285.

Claxton, A., Cramer, J., & Pierce, C. (2001). A systematic review of the associations
between dose regimens and medication compliance. *Clinical Therapist, 23*(8),
1296-1310.

Coambs, R., Jensen, P., Her, M., Ferguson, B., Jarry, J., & Wong, J. et al. (1995). Review
of the scientific literature on the prevalence, consequences, and health costs of noncompliance and innappropriate use of prescription medication in Canada. Toronto:
University of Toronto, 103-112.

Col, N., Fanale, J., & Kronholm, P. (1990). The role of mediation noncompliance and
adverse drug reactions in hospitalizations of the elderly. *Archives of Internal Medicine, 150*(4), 841-845.

Coons, S., Sheahan, S., Martin, S., Hendricks, J., Robbins, C., & Johnson, J. (1994).
Predictors of medication noncompliance in a sample of older adults. *Clinical Therapist, 16*(1), 110-117.

Cooper, J., Love, D., & Rafford, P. (1982). Intentional prescription nonadherence
(noncompliance) by the elderly. *Journal of the American Geriatrics Society, 30*(1),
329-333.

Cragill, J. (1992). Medication compliance in elderly people: Influencing variables and
interventions. *Journal of Advance Nursing, 17*(4), pp. 422-426.

Cramer, J. (1995). Microelectronic systems for monitoring and enhancing patient compliance with medication regimens. *Drugs, 49*(4), 321-327.

Cramer, J., Mattson, R., & Prevey, M. (1989). How often is medication taken as prescribed? A novel assessment technique. *Journal of the American Medical Association [JAMA], 261*(22), 3273-3277.

Cramer, J., Scheyer, R., & Mattson, R. (1990). Compliance declines between clinic visits. *Archives of Internal Medicine, 150*(7), 1509-1510.

Cramer, J., Vachon, L., & Desforges, C. (1995). Dose frequency and dose interval compliance with multiple antiepileptic medications during a controlled clinical trial. *Epilepsia, 36*(11), 1111-1117.

deKlerk, E. (2001). Patient compliance with enteric-coated weekly fluoxetine during continuation treatment of major depressive disorder. *Journal of Clinical Psychiatry, 62*(Supplement 22), 43-47.

Edelberg, H., Shallenberger, E., & Wei, J. (2000). One-year follow-up of medication management capacity in highly functioning older adults. *Journal of Gerontology, Series A, Biological Sciences/Medical Sciences, 55A*(10), M 550-M553.

Edwards, P. (1995). Teaching older patients about their medication. *Professional Nurse, 11*(3), 165-6.

Eisen, S., Miller, D., Woodward, R., Eisen, D., Miller; R., & Woodward, E. et al. (1990). The effect of prescribed daily dose frequency on patient medication compliance. *Archives of Internal Medicine, 150*(9), 1881-1884.

Feinstein, A. (1990). On white-coat effects and the electronic monitoring of compliance. *Archives of Internal Medicine, 150*(7), 1377-1378.

Fitten, L., Coleman, L., & Siembieda, D. (1995). Assessment of capacity to comply with medication regimens in older patients. *Journal of American Geriatric Society, 43*(3), 361-367.

Garfield, F., & Caro, J. (2000). Achieving patient buy-in and long term compliance with antihypertensive treatment. *Disease Management and Health Outcomes, 7*(1), 13-20.

Gazmararian, J., Baker, D., Williams, M., Parker, R, Scott, T., & Green, D. et al. (1999). Health literacy among Medicare enrollees in a managed care organization. *JAMA, 281*(6), 554-551.

Gilbert, A., Luszcz, M., & Owen, N. (1993). Medication use and its correlates among the elderly. *Austin Journal of Public Health, 17*(1), 18-22.

Gray, S., Mahoney, J., & Blough, D. (2001). Medication adherence in elderly patients receiving home health services following hospital discharge. *Annals of Pharmacotherapy, 35*(5), 539-545.

Greenberg, R. (1984). Overview of patient compliance with medication dosing: A literature review. *Clinical Therapist, 6*(5), 593-599.

Grymonpre, R., Mitenko, P., & Sitar, D. (1988). Drug-associated hospital admissions in elderly medical patients. *Journal of the American Geriatrics Society, 36*(9), 1092-1098.

Guthrie, R. (2001). The effects of postal and telephone reminders on compliance with pravastatin therapy in a national registry: Results of the first myocardial infarction risk reduction program. *Clinical Therapist, 23*(6), 970-980.

Haynes, R., McDonald, H., & Garg, A. (2002). Interventions for helping patients to follow prescriptions for medications. Cochrane Database. *Systematic Review, 2*, CD000011.

Hughes, C. (2004). Medication non-adherence in the elderly: How big is the problem? *Drugs and Aging, 21*(12), 793-811.

Hurd, P., & Blevins, J. (1984). Aging and the color of pills [letter]. *The New England Journal of Medicine, 31*(3), 202.

Hurd, P., & Butkovich, S. (1986). Compliance problems and the older patient: Assessing functional limitations. *Drug Intelligence and Clinical Pharmacy, 20*(7), 228-231.

Isacc, L., & Tamblyn, R. (1993). Compliance and cognitive function: A methodological approach to measuring unintentional errors on medication compliance in the elderly. McGill-Calgary Drug Research Team. JOURNAL33, pp. 772-781.

Keram, S., & Williams, S. (1988). Quantifying the ease or difficulty older persons experience in opening medication containers. *Journal of American Geriatrics Society, 36*(1),198-201.

Klein, D., Turvey, C., & Wallence, R. (2004). Elders who delay medication because of cost: health insurance, demographic, health, and financial correlates. *Gerontologist, 44*(6), 779-87.

Kruse, W. (1992). Patient compliance with drug treatment–New perspectives on an old problem. *Clinical Investigation, 70*(2),163-6.

Kruse, W., Eggert-Kruse, W., & Rampmaier, J. (1991). Dosage frequency and drug-compliance behavior: A comparative study on compliance with a medication to be taken twice or four times daily. *European Journal of Clinical Pharamacology, 41*(2), 589-592.

Kuzuya, M., Endo, H., Umegaki, H., Nakao, M., Niwa, T., & Kumagai, T. et al. (2000). Factors influencing noncompliance with medication regimens in the elderly. *Nippon Ronen Igakkai Zasshi, 37*(5), 363-70.

Lakshman, M., Fernando, M., & Kazarian, S. (1995). Patient education in the drug treatment of psychiatric disorders: Effect on compliance and outcome. *CNS Drugs, 3*(4), 291-304.

Lassila, H., Stoehr, G., Ganguli, M., Seaberg, E., Gilby, J., & Belle, S. et al. (1996). Use of prescription medications in an elder rural population: The MoVIES Project. *Annals of Pharamcotherapy, 30*(6), 589-595.

Lin, I., Spiga, R., & Fortsch, W. (1979). Insight and adherence to medication in chronic schizophrenics. *Journal of Clinical Psychiatry, 40*(3), 430-432.

MacLaughlin, E. Raehl, C., Treadway, A., Sterling, T., Zoller, D., & Bond, C. (2005). Assesing medication adherence in the elderly: Which tools to use in clinical practice? *Drugs Aging, 22*(3), 231-255.

McDonald, H., Garg, A., & Haynes, R. (2002). Interventions to enhance patient adherence to medication prescriptions. *Scientific Review, 22*(12), 2868-2879.

McKenney, J., & Harrison, W. (1976). Drug-related hospital admissions. *American Journal of Hospital Pharmacy, 33*(8) 792-795.

Meredith, P. (1996). Therapeutic implications of drug 'holidays.' *European Heart, 17*(Supplement A), 21-24.

Meyer, M., & Schuma, A. (1989). Assessment of geriatric patients' functional ability to take medication. *Drug Intelligence and Clinical Pharmacy, 23*(1), 171-174.

Mojtabai, R., & Olfson, M. (2003). Medication costs, adherence, and health outcomes among Medicare benificiaries. *Health Affairs, 22*(4), 220-229.

Monane, M., Bohn, R., & Gurwitz, J. (1996). Compliance with antihypertensive therapy among elderly Medicaid enrollees: The roles of age, gender and race. *American Journal of Public Health, 86*(11), 1805-1808.

Morrell, R., Park, D., & Poon, L. (1989). Quality of instruction on prescription drug labels: Effects on memory and comprehension in young and old adults. *Gerontologist, 29*(3), 345-354.

Morrell, P., Park, D., & Poon, L. (1990). Effects of labeling techniques on memory and comprehension of prescription information in young and old adults. *Journal of Gerontology, 45*(1), 166-172.

Morrow, D., Leirer, V., & Sheikh, J. (1988). Adherence and medication instructions: Review and recommendations. *Journal of American Geriatrics Society, 36*(9), 1147-1160.

Murray, M., Darnell, J., & Weinberger, M. (1986). Factors contributing to medication noncompliance in elderly public housing tenants. *Drug Intelligence and Clinical Pharmacy, 20*(2), 146-152.

Murray, M., Morrow, D., Weiner, M., Clark, D., Tu, W., & Deer, M. et al. (2001). Compliance and knowledge about prescribed medication among elderly home-care recipients by method of providing medications. *Nippon Ronen Igakkai Zasshi, 38*(5), 644-50.

National Center on Elder Abuse [NCEA] (2005). Abuse statistics. Retrieved August 20, 2005 from the World Wide Web at: http://www.elderabusecenter.org/default.cfm?p=abusestatistics.cfm

Paes, A., Bakker, A., & Soe-Agnie (1998). Measurement of patient compliance. *Pharmacy World & Science, 20*(2), 73-77.

Paris, W., Dunham, S., Sebastian, A., Jacobs, C., & Nour, B.(1999). Medication nonadherence and its relation to financial restriction. *Journal of Transplant Coordination, 9*(3), 149-152.

Park, D., Morrell, R., & Frieske, D. (1992). Medication adherence behaviors in older adults: Effects of external cognitive supports. *Psychology and Aging, 7*(3), 252-256.

Peterson, A., Takiya, L., & Finley, R. (2003). Meta-analysis of trials of interventions to improve medication adherence. *American Journal of Health-System Pharmacy, 60*(7), 657-665.

Pullar, T., Birtwell, A., & Wiles, P. (1988). Use of a pharmacologic indicator to compare compliance with tablets prescribed to be taken once, twice, or three times daily. *Clinical Pharmacology and Therapeutics, 44*(4), 540-545.

Pullar, T., Kumar, S., & Tindall, H. (1989). Time to stop counting the tablets? *Clinical Pharmacology, 46*(3), 163-168.

Pushpangadan, M., & Feely, M. (1998). Once a day is best: Evidence or assumption? The relationship between compliance and dosage frequency in older people. *Drugs and Aging, 13*(3), 223-227.

Raehl, C., Bond, C., Woods, T., Patry, R., & Sleeper, R. (2002). Individualized drug used assessment in the elderly. *Pharmacotherapy, 22*(10), 1239-1248.

Roter, D., Hall, J., & Merisca, R. (1998). Effectiveness of interventions to improve patient compliance: A meta-analysis. *Medical Care, 36*(12), 1138-1161.

Rudd, P., Byyny, R., & Zachary, V. (1989). The natural history of medication compliance in a drug trial: Limitations of pill counts. *Clinical Pharmacology and Therapeutics, 46*(2), 169-176.

Rudd, P., & Lenert, L. (1995). Pharmacokinetics as an aid to optimizing compliance with medications. *Clinical Pharmacokinetics, 28*(1), 1-6.

Ruscin, J., & Semla, T. (1996). Assessment of medication management skills in older outpatients. *Annals of Pharmacotherapy, 30*(12), 1083-1088.

Ryan, A. (1998). Medication compliance and older people: A review of the literature. *International Journal of Nursing Studies, 36*(2), 153-162.

Sackett, D., & Haynes, R. (1976). Compliance with therapeutic regimes. Baltimore: The John Hopkins University Press.

Salzman, C. (1995). Medication compliance in the elderly. *Journal of Clinical Psychiatry, 56*(*Supplement 1*), 18-22.

Schoen, M., DiDomenico, R., & Connor, S. (2001). Impact of the cost of prescription drugs on clinical outcomes in indigent patients with heart disease. *Pharamacotherapy, 21*(12), 1455-1463.

Scott, T., Gazmararian, J., & Williams, M. (2002). Health literacy and preventative health care use among Medicare enrollees in a managed care organization. *Medical Care, 40*(3), 395-404.

Secnik, K., Pathak, D., & Cohen, J. (2000). Postcard and telephone reminders for unclaimed prescriptions: A comparative evaluation using survival analysis. *Journal of American Pharmacological Association, 40*(2), 243-251.

Sharkness, C., & Snow, D. (1992). The patient's view of hypertension and compliance. *American Journal of Preventive Medicine, 8*(2), 141-146.

Shelton, P., Fritsch, M., & Scott, M. (2000). Assessing medication appropriateness in the elderly: a review of available measures. *Drugs Aging, 16*(6), 437-50.

Simkins, C., & Wenzloff, N. (1986). Evaluation of a computerized reminder system in the enhancement of patient medication refill compliance. *Drug Intelligence and Clinical Pharmacy, 20*(8), 799-802.

Steiner, A., Vetter, W., & Schweiz Rundsch, E. (1994). Patient compliance-concept formation, assessment methods. *Medical Praxis, 2*(31), 841-5.

Stewart, R. (1991). Noncompliance in the elderly: Is there a cure? *Drugs and Aging, 1*(2), 163-167.

Stewart, R., & Caranasos, G. (1989). Medication compliance in the elderly. *Medical Clinics of North America, 73*(6), 1551-1563.

Stockton, P., & Jones, J. (1993). Medication use by the elderly. *Aging (Milano), 5*(5), 337-47.

Taggart, A., Johnston, G., & McDevin, D. (1981). Does the frequency of daily dosage influence compliance with compliance with dixogin therapy? *British Journal of Clinical Pharmacology, 11*(1), 31-34.

Tinkelman, D., Vanderpool, G., & Carroll, M. (1980). Compliance differences following administration of theophylline at six-and twelve-hour intervals. *Annals of Allergy, 44*(4), 283-286.

Urquhart, J. (1994). Role of patient compliance in clinical pharmacokinetics: A review of recent research. *Clinical Pharmacokinetics, 27*(3), 202-215.

Urquhart, J., & Chevalley, C. (1988). Impact of unrecognized dosing errors on the cost and effectiveness of pharmaceuticals. *Drug Information Journal, 22*(3), 363-378.

van Eijken, M., Tsang, S., & Wensing, M. (2003). Interventions to improve medication compliance in older patients living in the community: a systematic review of the literature. *Drugs Aging, 20*(3), 229-40.

Vik, S., Maxwell, C., & Hogan, D. (2004). Measurement, correlates, and health outcomes of medication adherence among seniors. *The Annals of Pharmacotherapy,* *38*(2), 303-312.

Weinberger, M. (2004). A conceptual framework to study medication adherence in older adults. *American Journal of Geriatric Pharmacotherapy, 2*(1), 36-43.

Weintraub, S. (1990). Compliance in the elderly. *Clinical Geriatric Medicine, 6*(2), 445-52.

Willey, C., Redding, C., Stafford, J., Garfield, F., Geletko, S., & Flanigan, T. et al. (2000). Stages of change for adherence with medication regimens for chronic disease: Development and validation of a measure. *Clinical Therapeutics, 22*(7), 858-871.

doi:10.1300/J394v04n01_07

Undergraduate Research:
From Educational Policy
to Critical Thinking

Julia M. Watkins, PhD

SUMMARY. The undergraduate social work curriculum with its requirement of research content is well-positioned to enhance student capacity and practice effectiveness. Research content should move far beyond the conventional thinking as necessary but not critically important at the undergraduate level, to discussions of knowledge enhancement for practice and preparation for advanced education. This article suggests the directions for further thought and conversation. doi:10.1300/J394v04n01_08 *[Article copies available for a fee from The Haworth Document Delivery Service: 1-800-HAWORTH. E-mail address: <docdelivery@haworth press.com> Website: <http://www.HaworthPress.com> © 2007 by The Haworth Press, Inc. All rights reserved.]*

KEYWORDS. Undergraduate social work, curriculum, research

Julia M. Watkins is Executive Director, Council on Social Work Education, 1725 Duke Street, Suite 500, Alexandria, VA 22314.

[Haworth co-indexing entry note]: "Undergraduate Research: From Educational Policy to Critical Thinking." Watkins, Julia M. Co-published simultaneously in *Journal of Evidence-Based Social Work* (The Haworth Press, Inc.) Vol. 4, No. 1/2, 2007, pp. 121-128; and: *Building Excellence: The Rewards and Challenges of Integrating Research into the Undergraduate Curriculum* (ed: Catherine N. Dulmus, and Karen M. Sowers) The Haworth Press, 2007, pp. 121-128. Single or multiple copies of this article are available for a fee from The Haworth Document Delivery Service [1-800-HAWORTH, 9:00 a.m. - 5:00 p.m. (EST). E-mail address: docdelivery@haworthpress.com].

Available online at http://jebsw.haworthpress.com
© 2007 by The Haworth Press, Inc. All rights reserved.
doi:10.1300/J394v04n01_08

INTRODUCTION

Discussions about research in the academy most frequently focus attention on the work of Master's and doctoral students and their research faculty. In fact, numerous institutions of higher education are mission and financially driven by the prestige of their faculty research portfolios including funding from external sources as well as their ability to attract even more prestigious faculty and therefore graduate students who will contribute to an inquiry based enterprise (Allen-Meares, 2005). There are, however, compelling arguments for a substantial emphasis on research at the undergraduate level of education in general and in social work education in particular. After all, the minds and critical abilities of future generations of practitioners, scholars and teachers are formed at least by the end of the undergraduate educational experience. In social work specifically, baccalaureate graduates become the practitioners on the front line of service provision–what they do must be based in solid research evidence and they must know how to understand that evidence and in the best of possible practice settings, carry out research based in their day-to-day practice.

There is increasing focus on undergraduate research throughout our institutions of higher education in the United States (Dotterer, 2002). This can be seen from the variety of initiatives over the last two decades from, for example, the National Science Foundation (NSF) programs seeking to integrate research and education from its Division of Undergraduate Education (Fortenberry, 1998; National Science Foundation [NSF], 1996) and the Council on Undergraduate Research (CUR). In 1996, the National Science Foundation conducted a review of undergraduate education. This review found that the work of the Division of Undergraduate Education was making progress and reported: "It is important to assist [undergraduate students] to learn not only science facts but, just as important, the methods and processes of research, what scientists and engineers do, how to make informed judgments about technical matters, and how to communicate and work in teams to solve complex problems."

The NSF program is science and engineering based, as opposed to the social sciences, while the focus of CUR and its related programs has been more on the natural science disciplines, but with an increasing interest in the social and behavioral sciences, as well as education at the undergraduate level. These latter disciplines, which include social work, are part of the development of a larger academic culture that prepares undergraduates to evaluate practice, broadly speaking. If the literature is an indication of location, the research activity has been primarily in the liberal arts colleges. The Council on Undergraduate Research (CUR) (see www.cur.org) is in the forefront of promoting undergraduate research and especially uses the model of faculty to student mentoring as a primary vehicle to accomplish its research educational agenda. Gates, Teller, Bernat, and Delgado (1998) suggest, "Professor-student interaction increases the persistence of students especially if students begin their research work early in their career" (p. 1133).

If there is consensus among the educational community, and specifically among faculty in social work education, that research at the undergraduate level is important, then what prompts this consensus and what is the direct applicability to the social work student and to the undergraduate social work curriculum? One answer is more obvious than others; it is certainly no secret that research is a knowledge derivative addressed in the unified approach to the Educational Policy and Accreditation Standards (EPAS) promulgated by the Council on Social Work Education (CSWE) (Council on Social Work Education, 2001). This may serve as a point of departure for our discussion, even though educational policy, beyond how it has been translated into accreditation standards, is possibly not the most important point or the first point of focus. It is at the programmatic level, in terms of goals and objectives and educational philosophy where an energetic discussion should be taking place. But even then to address only the programmatic level, however a seemingly appropriate step would be a misstep without first framing the discussion and analysis firmly in the intrinsic goals and outcomes of a higher education as well as the specific institutional context. The reader is urged to review the literature coming out of CUR to get a sense of this movement at the institutional level.

The structural domain for undergraduate level social work education is preparation of graduates for generalist professional practice. And within this structural framework, the Educational Policy (EP) statement outlines program objectives that guide the construction and delivery of the curriculum. Relative to research at the undergraduate level the most salient points to note in terms of program objectives (EP 3) (Council on Social Work Education, 2001, p. 7) distilled and presented here in an abbreviated format (italics added) are:

- Social work education is grounded in the *liberal arts*
- Program objectives–apply *critical thinking* skills
- Program objectives–use *theoretical frameworks* supported by *empirical evidence*

- Program objectives–*analyze,* formulate, and influence social policies
- Program objectives–*evaluate research* studies, *apply research findings* to practice, and *evaluate* practice interventions

Moreover, the Educational Policy Statement (EP) specifically addresses research as a foundation curriculum content area (EP 4.6): "Qualitative and quantitative research content provides understanding of a scientific, analytic, and ethical approach to building knowledge for practice. The content prepares students to develop, use, and effectively communicate empirically based knowledge, including evidence-based interventions. Research knowledge is used by students to provide high-quality services; to initiate change; to improve practice, policy, and social service delivery; and to evaluate their own practice" (Council on Social Work Education [CSWE], 2001, p. 10). Baccalaureate level educational programs are required under the Accreditation Standards (AS 2; and B2.0.1) (CSWE, 2001, p. 12) to define their conceptions of generalist practice as well as describe their coverage of the professional foundation curriculum as spelled out in EP 4, including the research content (EP 4.6) (CSWE, 2001, p. 10).

The conclusion, not surprisingly, is unequivocal. Research is an important, in fact a required component of the undergraduate curriculum. Without such content clearly described and outcomes demonstrated, the program would be found out of compliance with accreditation standard B 2.0.1 (CSWE, 2001, p. 12).

It is importantly notable that nothing within EPAS specifies prescriptively how a program will develop and deliver this research component, only that it must do so. Hopefully, the consensus among faculty is motivated by more than the Accreditation Standards. This is precisely why programs and their faculties, within the context of their institutional mission and purposes, may exercise leadership in the creative and innovative design of research content.

Preparation of the undergraduate level social work practitioner is both an enormously burdensome as well as an immensely gratifying professional responsibility. Exercising creativity and innovativeness while at the same time searching for the "right" formula, the ultimate curriculum design–if there is such a thing–in that preparation is a constant challenge to the social work faculty. Nevertheless, if our basic purpose is the preparation of those baccalaureate level practitioners, leaving aside for a moment the preparation for education at an advanced level, we unmask at least three important questions to stimulate future content and pedagogical discourse.

1. What are the elements of the liberal arts with specific implications for the undergraduate social work curriculum?
2. How do students most effectively learn to conceptualize and ask "good" research questions and how do they most effectively learn the application of the skills of research?
3. What is the process by which students come to analyze and understand the products of research and apply such understandings in their social work practice?

The answers to these questions require broad-based discussion among all of social work education. To the experienced educator, however, discussion themes in response to these questions are already part of the everyday discussion on List serves and at annual conferences of the Baccalaureate Program directors (BPD) and the CSWE Annual Program Meeting. The purpose served in this brief text is to further frame the future discussion. Three themes are identified that emerge when informal discussion of the questions takes place.

The liberal arts (and sciences) involves developing the habits of mind that prompt students, and later practitioners, to think in critical terms, to problem solve, to create new propositions and positions, to communicate and persuade, to exercise flexibility as well as rigorous intellectual discipline in understanding global as well as local events, to generate and think in terms of ideas (as opposed to ideology), to understand the process of science, to engage in the process of discovery, and to do so responsibly and ethically. In a recent presentation, Kay Hoffman, President of the Council on Social Work Education, suggested the key ideas to be incorporated in undergraduate education, many of them a direct derivative of the liberal arts (and sciences): "science of inquiry; ethical imperatives; diversity and difference based both in cultural studies and in the deontological questions of meaning and experience; assessment that focuses on questions of human conduct and human nature–how do we get to be the way we are–and engagement with the community-global and local" (Hoffman, 2005).

A second theme that experienced educators seem to address is the nature of the faculty/student relationship in this research enterprise as a way of cutting into the second question (Lopatto, 2003). Mentoring is seen as primary to the success of the advanced student, particularly within doctoral education. But it also is an important component of the undergraduate research experience. Students learn from their faculty–the good habits of mind, and they also understand when good habits of mind are underdeveloped or in short supply. In the smaller liberal arts schools, there is greater opportunity to anchor student research and its attendant skill development in interdisciplinary projects, working with faculty from social work and other disciplines.

Complimentary to the mentor/student relationship is the nature of research projects in which the student and mentor are engaged. The opportunity to connect the research to the educational field component and therefore engage the student in a community-based research project is a decided asset of social work education. It does, however, require a highly integrated approach to faculty deployment as well as integrative knowledge development in order to ensure successful outcomes of asking good questions and skill application.

A third theme seems to engage discussion about the nature of the social work student population and the responsibility of the faculty to promote life-long learning and the acquisition and application of new knowledge. Given the current complexity of our student populations, the structures or our institutions of higher education, the cost of obtaining a higher education degree, and the pragmatic need to have a job at the end of the degree, the liberal arts, or the general education requirements, as well as specific research courses, are seen as something to "get out of the way" quickly so as to get on to the real essence of the educational program, i.e., social work practice and its applications. The challenge to the faculty is to discover, and it is a process of discovery guided by some general principles of learning theory, the pedagogical mechanisms within the social work curriculum that will promote student incorporation of a life-long process of relating research to practice and acquisition of new knowledge.

The "set aside" in this text has been the undergraduate experience as preparation for advanced level education, i.e., Master's and doctoral education. Defining and ensuring sound educational objectives and outcomes, including research capability at the undergraduate level, is the fundamental educational precursor to success at the advanced level. In the same presentation, Hoffman (2005) connected the ideas from the undergraduate curriculum to the content needs in doctoral education where research skills of methodology, analysis, moral decision making and dissemination are dominant, showing clearly the importance of the liberal arts (and sciences) as well as research in the undergraduate curriculum to its importance as a grounding for advanced study where preparation of the next generation of faculty scholars and leaders in social work education takes place.

If we must be further persuaded or convinced to maintain a consensus beyond accreditation standards for the inclusion of research in the undergraduate curriculum, some interesting work in support of the "essential benefits" has been reported in a study reported by David Lopatto (2003). In a survey of college faculty, Lopatto found that the top 6 benefits were judged to be: learn a topic area in depth; construct meaningful problem; learn to use appropriate methodology; learn to work and think independently; learn to design solutions to problems; and improve oral communication skills (Lopatto, 2003, p. 141). In the same study, Lopatto reported the findings of student responses about the most important benefits of an undergraduate research experience. The top 6 were: enhancement of professional or academic credentials; clarification of a career path; understanding the research process in your field; learning a topic in depth; developing a continuing relationship with a faculty member; and learning to work independently (Lopatto, 2003, p. 142).

Our challenge then as social work educators is to move beyond the EPAS requirement of research content and our acknowledgement that social work education is grounded in the liberal arts, to engage in a robust and spirited conversation about the values and benefits of research in the undergraduate curriculum–the benefits to the institution, the faculty and the students and ultimately social work practice. The liberal arts and sciences and its concomitant of critical thinking and analysis should be a focal point for this discussion as we seek ways to enhance student knowledge and preparation for intellectual leadership in the profession.

REFERENCES

Allen-Meares, P. (2005, Fall). The role of social work education in the academy. *Social Work Education Reporter, 53*(3), 1, 17.

Council on Social Work Education. (2001). *Educational Policy and Accreditation Standards.* Alexandria, VA: Author.

Dotterer, R. L. (2002). Student-faculty collaborations, undergraduate research, and collaboration as an administrative model. *New Directions for Teaching and Learning, 90,* 81-89.

Fortenberry, N. L. (1998, December). Integration of research and curriculum. *Council on Undergraduate Research Quarterly,* 54-61. Retrieved September 29, 2005, from the Council on Undergraduate Research website at http://www.cur.org/governmt.html

Gates, A. Q., Teller, P. J., Bernat, A., Delgado, N., & Della-Piana, C. K. (1998). Meeting the challenge of expanding participation in the undergraduate research experience. *Proceedings from the 1998 Frontiers in Education Conference, Tempe, AZ,* 1133-1138. Retrieved November 21, 2005, from http://fie.engrng.pitt.edu/fie98/papers/1212.pdf.

Hoffman, K. (2005, November). *The intersection between undergraduate education and doctoral education in social work.* Presentation at the Baccalaureate Social Work Education Conference, Austin, TX.

Lopatto, D. (2003, March). The essential features of undergraduate research. *Council on Undergraduate Research Quarterly,* 139-142.

The National Science Foundation. (1996). *Shaping the future: New expectations for undergraduate education in Science, Mathematics, Engineering, and Technology* (Document number NSF 96-139). Arlington, VA: Author. Retrieved November 21, 2005, from http://www.nsf.gov/pubs/stis1996/nsf96139/nsf96139.txt

doi:10.1300/J394v04n01_08

Index

Abuse
  childhood and psychopathology in
    adulthood, 63-65
  childhood and suicidal behavior,
    61-78. *See also* Suicidal
    behavior
  mental, 66-67,66t,72t
  physical, 66-67,66t,69-70,69t
  sexual, 27-45,65-66,65t,68-69,68t.
    See also Sexually abused
    children
Academic Bill of Rights. *See* Brower
    Report
Age
  medication adherence and, 98-100.
    See also Medication
    adherence
  sensitivity to medication and, 100
Assisted living facilities
  as compared with nursing homes,
    48-49
  conclusion, 57-58
  data collection, 52
  dementia patients and stress, 50-51
  discussion, 56-57
  European studies, 50
  growth rate, 48
  measurements, 52-53
  method, 52-54
  results, 54-55,55t
  sample, 54
  sources of staff stress and strain, 50
  staff duties, 49-50
  stress and strain in personal care
    assistants, 47-59
  study background and rationale,
    48-51
  study hypotheses, 51

Brower Report, 1-9
  college/university obligations, 2-3
  recommendations for change, 4-6
  student rights, 2-3
*Built to Last: Successful Habits of
    Visionary Companies*
    (Collins & Porras), 12

Carnegie Foundation for the
    Advancement of Teaching, 2
Cassie, Kimberly McClure, 47-59
Childhood abuse. *See* Abuse
Children, sexually abused, 27-45. *See
    also* Sexually abused children
Closing of the American Mind
    (Bloom), 2
Community, sense of, 5
Council for Social Work Education,
    121-128
Council for Undergraduate Research,
    122
  Baccalaureate Program directors,
    125
  Brower Report and, 8
  Educational Policy Statement,
    121-128
Court-mandated treatment
  data analysis, 91-92
  data collection, 91
  discussion, 93-94
  juvenile deliquency studies, 81-82
  juvenile recidivism and, 79-95
  literature review, 81-89
  method, 89-91
  practice implications, 94
  research question, 89
  results, 92-93,92t,93t

   129